COUNTRY VET

You'd think it was the easiest thing in the world to get a dog and a bitch to mate . . .

Eventually, with the panting owner holding on to the bitch's head, I took hold of the dog's two hind legs and lifted him into position. Success appeared to be imminent, but after several minutes my arms were tired and aching. Though he appeared to be capable of sustaining the pace, I was not. To relieve my arms of the tension, I kneeled down carefully, not wishing to distract him. He took my change of posture in his stride.

I remained in the kneeling position, holding a paw in each hand to stop them slipping off my thighs and bent forward over their backs. I felt as though I was taking an active part in the production of a canine 'blue' film. My embarrassment was not lessened by an audience of several village dogs watching the proceedings avidly from the other side of the garden fence.

The climax of my embarrassment came when the bitch turned her head to one side and looked at the dog with apparent indifference. She then turned her head to the other side, looked me in the eye and, with gentle affection, gave me a long wet lick across the face.

Country Vet

Denis Farrier

CORONET BOOKS
Hodder and Stoughton

Printed and bound in Great Britain for
Coronet Books, Hodder and Stoughton, London
by Richard Clay (The Chaucer Press) Ltd,
Bungay, Suffolk

ISBN 0 340 18638 0

For Beany and other bitches

CONTENTS

CHAPTER ONE

STUDENT VET

AMID the throng of students at the Veterinary College, I felt, as a member of the First Year, conspicuously gauche and innocent. We wore stiffly starched, new white laboratory coats, neatly buttoned up the front. We carried text books fresh from the book shop, and virginal notebooks. Second and Third Year students were distinguished by the exotic botanical and biological stains, worn as a badge of knowledge on their frayed and well-used coats. The top button was usually left unfastened. Fourth and Final Year swung confidently along the corridors, white coats flapping open and a stethoscope dangling nonchalantly from a pocket. The occasional blood stain enhanced their stature.

After the enforced teaching discipline of school, I found it difficult to adjust myself to the apparently casual attitude at college. Lectures could be missed and a pleasant hour spent in the canteen, drinking coffee and sorting out the future policy of the veterinary profession as a whole. There being no standard to go by, I found it difficult to judge how hard I should work. Worldly wise, experienced Second Year students led us to believe that any form of work was quite superfluous. One passed exams as a matter of course. I was unwilling to accept their reassurances and probably worked far harder than was necessary. Life as a First Year student was worrying.

I found Chemistry and Physics a bore. In Biology the sectioning and drawing of a tomato and the stem of a plant all neatly labelled in my botanical note-book, seemed totally at variance with the image of myself as a venerated veterinary surgeon, the pillar of some rural community.

The dissection of the earthworm, in Practical Zoology, with the exposure of its intimate habits and sex life, did little to encourage me. The cockroach was better, at least it had legs. The dogfish, in all respects a miniature shark, was interesting from a zoological point of view. I would spend hours poring over its detailed anatomy, with eyes watering from the pungent fumes of the formalin in which it had been preserved. It became less attractive when I was given fish and chips for supper by my landlady and I found, under the pseudonym of Rock Salmon and a thick layer of tomato ketchup, that I was once more dissecting dogfish.

The advent of the rabbit on my dissecting board was a major step forward. It was a mammal, warm-blooded, and its sexual habits bore a marked similarity to those of the veterinary student.

After the rabbit, we were subjected to the acute mental trauma of the yearly examination. Most of us succeeded and carried our inflated little egos through to the Second Year. Our white coats had lost their sheen, our note-books were well worn and dog-eared. We were able to pick out the new First Year students and, with studied benevolence, exercise our new superiority.

Physiology, the study of the functioning of various organs, had its lighter moments. A frog's heart, still beating, had a minute glass canula inserted into its main vein. Fixed on to a stand, it was supplied with *Ringers* solution, a mixture of salts similar to those found in the blood. A small hook, attached to the apex, was connected to a lever. We measured the rate and strength of the heart beats and they were recorded by the end of the lever on a revolving drum of smoked paper. The effects of various cardiac stimulants and depressants, which were added to the *Ringers* solution could be observed and recorded on the drum. Sabotage of one's neighbour's efforts, if he was careless enough to leave his apparatus unguarded and slide off to the lavatory, always caused a diversion. Strong black coffee, from the canteen, with or without sugar, added to the fluid in his carefully controlled experiment, caused the most remarkable convulsions of the lever. Long, sweeping marks flashed briefly across the smoked paper on his drum, to end up with a few stutters and a dull straight line as the heart died an unnatural death.

Parasitology, involving the study of internal worms—hook, round and tape—was tedious. But our lecturer was dedicated to the subject. He had a pale, dome-shaped head with almost circular ears which resembled the suckers on the head of the tapeworm. His nick-name, inevitably, was 'Scolex', it being the correct scientific name for the head of a tapeworm. His enthusiasm was unbounded. He spent much time at the blackboard, with coloured chalks, drawing in the most intricate detail the insides of segments of tapeworms and liver flukes. Certain liver flukes, he pointed out, were distinguished by the fact that the testes were not side by side, but in tandem. One student deferentially raised a hand.

'Sir, is that why, the testes being in tandem, it is referred to as the "sexual cycle"?'

'Scolex' was a tolerant man and had had considerable experience in the handling of students. His answer was brief.

'Like so many tapeworm segments, I shall allow your query to fall on stony ground.'

Veterinary Anatomy, the dissection of the horse and cow, offered plenty of scope to the less serious-minded student. 'Flesh fights' were common, there being plenty of ammunition available. Apart from the one I was working on, there were three other horses in the vast, white-tiled Dissection Room. They were strapped on their backs on low metal tables, their stiffened legs pointing to the lofty ceiling. They were well spaced out in the centre of the room. Dogs and cats, on smaller tables, occupied one side of the room. The other side, facing north, was like an artist's studio, one large expanse of glass. Bones and unusual anatomical specimens in glass jars, lined one end. The space at the other end was taken up by washbasins and sinks.

Fourteen students worked round each horse cadaver. Two on each leg, two on the head and neck, two on the chest or thorax and two on the abdomen. One day, my careful isolation and drawing of the tendons and ligaments of the fore-leg of the horse, was interrupted by a large lump of wet liver, which hit me below the right ear, slid down the front of my shirt and

11

blotted my copy-book.

I thought that the offending piece of liver, bearing in mind the accuracy of the shot, had come from the next table. The liver being situated in the abdomen, I figured that the two abdominal dissectionists were responsible. They may have loaned it as ammunition to one of the others, but, being accessories before, during and after the fact, they were guilty.

I observed them at length. Both of them were obviously dedicated students of anatomy. Their heads were bent low in earnest concentration on their allotted tasks.

To show them that I would have no part in churlish horse-play, I tossed the piece of liver into a nearby waste-bin. Rupert, my immediate neighbour, was working on the head and neck. He had removed one eyeball, made detailed drawings of all its aspects and listed the muscles which, in life, controlled its movements. Having no further use for it, he quietly passed it across to me and concentrated on his horse's nostril.

I waited until the professor of Veterinary Anatomy and his assistant were occupied at the far end of the room. With an unerring aim, I shied the eyeball at the next table. I missed but only the two abdominal students ducked.

It was some days later that Rupert and I were pottering about on the banks of a river. We discovered a dead water rat. Our training in Zoology had not deserted us. We took it back to the College and dissected it in the bathroom. Being keen students, the fact that it had been dead for a long time did not deter us. It was a male water rat and it had two well developed testicles. Presumably due to the decomposition, they were of a greenish-white hue. Simultaneously we realised the possibilities. With a grin we placed them in a matchbox for safe-keeping.

Each Friday, the college canteen used to serve small, tinned, greenish-white grapes at lunch time as a dessert. Rupert and I casually took our places at lunch on either side of one of the students who had hit me with the liver. The main course was fried liver. Afterwards we had cheese. He chose the grapes. A touch on his arm from Rupert diverted his attention. I emptied the contents of the matchbox on to his plate and they merged

12

in completely. We watched him as he emptied his plate and spooned up all the juice

Retaliation against the other student was in a different manner. Long balloons made of thin rubber could be obtained. Affluent students bought them in packets of three, others retrieved them, 'second-hand' from the nearby river. These could be filled with a pint or more of water. In the laboratories there was a wide range of botanical dyes and biological stains. Mixed with the water in the balloons, it added a splash of colour to the considerable impact as the device hit the pavement. From the college roof, five stories above the ground level, a few practice drops using balloons half filled with plain water were made. As our timing and aim improved, a few perplexed and one or two irate passers-by stopped and looked up as their boots got splashed. For the actual attack we used three balloons. The water in one coloured with Gentian Violet, one with Brilliant Green and the other with orange-red Safranin. Our target was fairly easily distinguished, as he affected to wear a 'deer-stalker' hat. He was of regular habits, lunched out and returned to college in good time for the two o'clock lecture. The Gentian Violet went wide of the target. The Safranin splashed his boots and the Brilliant Green was a direct hit, glancing off his ridiculous hat and exploding on his shoulder. We retreated, chuckling, from the roof.

We took our places in the lecture room and watched the door avidly for his multi-hued appearance. We were disappointed but not unduly surprised that he didn't turn up. He had either slunk off home or was trying to clean himself up in the cloakroom.

He attended the three o'clock lecture. He appeared to be quite composed and, to our disappointment, though we eyed him carefully, quite unblemished. A series of notes passed across the lecture room established the fact that he had missed his bus and regrettably had to miss the first lecture.

The three o'clock lecture was interrupted by one of the college porters who handed a note to the lecturer. He read the note, coughed lightly and scanned the room with steely eyes.

'A new member of the college staff, the Assistant Demonstrator in Animal Husbandry, was this afternoon subjected to an unwarranted attack. The Principal intends to find out who was responsible and to punish them severely.'

During the final year at college, we studied Veterinary Surgery and Veterinary Medicine. In these subjects we could apply the detailed basic facts that we had, or should have, assimilated in the previous four years. It was necessary to fall back on this knowledge in order to form an accurate diagnosis and to prescribe the correct treatment. Looking back from my position as a Final Year student, I was now able to appreciate that the absorption of un-interesting facts, though dull, had not been a waste of time.

Most of the work at the college was on theory. Experience of the practical aspects of Surgery and Medicine was gained by spending the vacation time with a practising veterinary surgeon. I learned how to inject a cow without breaking the hypodermic needle and without getting kicked. I learned many things which were vital to success and even survival as a veterinary surgeon.

One of the more important, less obvious, aspects being the care and handling of difficult and disgruntled clients.

It became increasingly clear to me that the success of a veterinary surgeon was based on much more than good diagnosis and correct treatment. A hesitant, unsympathetic or impatient approach to the client would affect his confidence and co-operation. Even if the treatment was successful, it would not always be appreciated. Under a cool, calm and competent exterior, many doubts could be hidden. A mistaken diagnosis could be glossed over. Even unsuccessful treatment would be forgiven and the owner's sympathy drawn away from his unfortunate animal.

I learnt all this mainly from the Vet who used to visit my uncle's farm in Devon, where as a boy I spent the long summer holidays. It was here that this story was born and my vocation decided.

14

CHAPTER TWO

THE FARM DOGS

MY uncle told me to take Gyp and Sport, the two farm dogs, and move a bunch of his Devon Longwool ewes and their black-faced Suffolk ram from Eighteen Acre Down. They had been grazing on stubble and he wanted them moved to another field called Long Meadow. It was a permanent pasture and, apart from palatable grass, it grew reeds, docks and a few thistles. A stream ran down its centre, bordered by more reeds. Damp and often waterlogged, it provided a bite for the ewes at the end of a long dry summer and was home for a pair of snipe.

As we approached, they took off from the reeds and jinked their way down the stream until they settled down to a steady flight path. Had I wanted to shoot them, this was the time to squeeze the trigger. Gyp, the Border collie, was only interested in sheep, chickens and in-season bitches, and barely acknowledged their departure. Sport, an aged yet willing springer spaniel, knew that I was not carrying a gun and realised that he would be wasting his time if he showed too much enthusiasm. When he was younger, he would have taken off, ears flapping, in eager, futile pursuit. He was older and wiser now and chose to conserve his energy.

Having checked that the gate at the far end of the meadow was shut and latched, the dogs and I returned to the farmyard. To the noise, dust and clatter of the threshing tackle. The dogs flopped down in the dust and cat-napped. My uncle, well over twenty stone of him, gave me a hard inquisitive look. I quickly nodded my head and returned to my job at the dirty end of the threshing machine.

During my first week at the farm, I had taken the same bunch of ewes up to Eighteen Acre Down. I had returned, well pleased with myself, even though Gyp had done all the work. Two hours later, the shepherd found that Eighteen Acre Down was empty. The gate at the far end of the field had been left open. The other side of the gate was 150 acres of moorland and scrub, only used for rough shooting. I was informed that my behaviour and lack of common sense was to be expected from day-trippers and picnickers, but it was inexcusable in anyone who thought he wanted to live and work in the country. I was told to take both dogs and not allowed to return until all forty ewes and the ram were back and secured in their field.

Some two hours later, scratched and bedraggled, I arrived with the sheep at the gateway. The dogs held them there and I counted thirty-nine ewes and one ram through into the field. Hoping that I'd miscounted, I rounded them up again into a corner of the field. One by one they were allowed to escape past me until thirty-nine and the ram had gone.

Hungry, tired and on the verge of tears, I stumped out of the gateway on to the moorland again. I had to find that one ewe in 150 acres of scrub.

Dejectedly, I pushed on through the waist-high bracken, with both dogs paddling along behind.

Gyp was an independent dog. He was content to work and neither asked for nor gave affection. The brief touch of a cold nose on the back of my hand gave me new confidence. I began to see why the sheep held him in such high esteem, why they were content to bow to his gentle authority. I held my head higher and was glad that I was alone with the dogs; a fellow human would have offered me either contempt or pity— neither of which would have found a lost sheep.

Sport, apparently, was an amiable and flannelled fool, except when working with a gun. On this occasion, sensing, as Gyp did, my inadequacy, he was prepared to use his nose on my behalf.

He tracked along the down-wind boundary of the moorland, Gyp and I followed respectfully behind. Several times, he paused, turned his nose up-wind and then padded on. The droppings and tufts of torn fleece left by the other thirty-nine ewes offered many false trails.

We found her on her back in a ditch, unable to right herself. She would have remained there and died. I heaved her upright but failed to hold her. She bolted into the bracken, to be headed off and held still by Gyp. Having lost the rest of the flock, she had also lost all sense of direction. As I approached her she bolted again. Gyp took off once more, brought her round and held her against a barrier of blackthorn scrub. In her stubborn panic she was not going to be led or driven.

I grabbed her, one hand under her neck, the other over her loins, holding on to the thick oily fleece. She was too heavy to be carried. I tried pulling her and she pulled back. When I pushed, she dug her toes in. I left her guarded by Gyp and cut a six-foot length of ash sapling. I trimmed off the side shoots except for one at the base, which I left about six inches long.

Wielding my home-fashioned shepherd's crook, I returned to the ewe, still held, panting, against the thorn bush by a crouching, watchful Gyp. I caught one of the ewe's hind legs with the crook and she took off on the other three, pulling against me and in a reasonably straight line. Gyp gave me a brief glance, which may have been admiration, but was probably relief that this pitifully stupid human was at last beginning to learn. I had missed my lunch and now it was nearly tea-time. I was hungry and tired, but much happier.

We reached the gate into Eighteen Acre Down, and I shut and latched it behind us and let the ewe go free. She lifted her head and looked around uncertainly. The rest of the flock were not in sight. I assumed they would be at the far end of the field, hidden by the rising ground in front of us. She'd find her companions soon enough and we left her wandering about in circles.

We mounted the rise and the rest of the field came into view. It was empty. Gyp's ears flattened on to his head and his easy gait faltered. I stopped and looked with dismay, bordering on panic, at the open gateway at the end of the field.

If they had turned right, they would have gone up the lane and out on the main road. They could now be five miles away in any of several directions. The thought was too monstrous to contemplate. I turned left down the lane towards the farm.

The dogs followed quietly behind me.

The farmyard, with its neat, new cornricks, was empty except for a few contented hens and a rooster. Gyp shot past me, ears forward and alert, up the lane towards the farmhouse garden. Sport and I followed at a shaggy trot. There seemed to be a lot more than thirty-nine ewes and one ram on the neatly tended lawn. They were browsing happily in the herbaceous border, which was my aunt's pride and the secret envy of the other members of the Women's Institute. Gyp, unable to appreciate the finer qualities of prize delphinium blooms, tore round behind them. With angry nips at their hocks, he hustled them towards the narrow garden gate. It was at this moment that my uncle and aunt returned from a shopping expedition.

The next few weeks I spent in the back-breaking and tedious chore of hoeing endless lines of mangolds. I was then transferred to threshing corn.

The turn-ups of my old school trousers were filled with barley awns and fluff. My boots were dusty, the trousers had once been clean and neatly pressed and I had spent many hours with the handle of a toothbrush and a lot of spit, boning the leather of the boots until they had shone like black glass.

Now, with a sweat-stained khaki shirt, they were my farm uniform. They represented freedom from the discipline of the old school tie and cap.

The dust, hanging on the sunlight, vibrated with the noise from the threshing machine. The snorting steam traction engine had towed it to the farm and had coaxed it into position between two ricks. It now stood back and supplied from its spinning fly-wheel the power for the snaking black pulley belt.

The owner of the threshing tackle and his mate, who was also fireman and water-carrier, were formally attired. They wore black and greasy overalls with striped, collarless shirts fastened at the neck with a shiny brass collar-stud. When they removed their equally black and greasy caps to scratch their heads, they showed, in contrast to their leathery, sunburnt features, indecently white, shining bald pates, with dark lank strands of sweaty hair.

They worked on top of the machine, cut the twine which

bound the sheaves and fed them into the whirling drum which beat the corn out of the ears. The supply of sheaves was pitch-forked to them by the men working on top of the diminishing ricks.

At ground level, at one end was the outlet for the corn. Four heavy duty 'West of England' sacks were clamped on to the corn shutes. When full, they were humped on to the scales to be counter-balanced, in the case of wheat, with two and a quarter hundredweight and an empty sack to make things equal. A sack of barley was weighed out at two hundred-weight, and oats, a mere hundredweight and a half. The full sacks were then stitched up with a sack needle and binder-twine and stacked in dog-eared rows to await loading and transport to the barn or to the local corn dealer, if the price was right.

Apart from the brief interlude with the sheep, I worked at the other, and dirty end of the machine. The chaff, awns, dried thistles and docks were discarded at my end and had to be raked clear and formed into a separate heap. Later, when all the ricks in the yard had been demolished and the fire risk lessened, it would be set on fire and left to smoulder for weeks.

At the end of a day's threshing my hair and eyebrows were grey with dust. My armpits and other sensitive portions of my anatomy were reddened and irritated by chaff and creeping barley awns.

The wooden top of the thresher, where the owner and his mate worked, was smooth, shiny and dangerously slippery, polished by the sheaves of corn which continually hit and slid across its surface. Working on this surface, with the corn underfoot, was like standing on a stainless steel table covered with ball-bearings.

Less than a month later, headlines in the local paper pro-claimed that the mate on the threshing tackle had lost an arm...

The level of the rick was still higher than the top of the thresher. Pitching from the rick at this stage was easy; two sheaves at a time could be slung down. The hard work came when they were down to ground level. Then the sheaves had to be tossed up ten or twelve feet, and if you didn't make it, they had to be tossed again.

He'd cut the cord on a sheaf and was feeding it into the drum when he was hit in the back by two sheaves at once. He dropped his knife, a treasured possession, tried to catch it and slipped.

Small pieces of finger and a shirt sleeve button came down the corn shute. The larger pieces, lumps of bone and long strands of blood-stained shirt came out with the dust and chaff.

On another occasion, the team work was interrupted by the vet. He had been asked to call the next time he was passing to castrate three young bull calves. My uncle reckoned that it would be cheaper than calling him out on a special visit. Once more, I was taken off the 'dust heap' and told to help him.

The calves, two months old, were chunky, well-muscled, pure-bred Devons with sleek red-brown coats. They eyed us speculatively as we approached their loose-box. I shot back the iron bolt on their door. They wheeled on their hocks and scampered like playful children to the far corner. They turned and faced us again, ears forward, eyes dark and wide with apprehension. The vet stood at the doorway. He held a large lump of cotton-wool soaked in antiseptic in one hand and a shining scalpel in the other. I walked straight up to them, talking softly. They bolted to another corner of the box and stood watching me with a little more confidence and some defiance. This time, I fixed my eyes on the left-hand one of the three and started to walk towards him. As he moved away I changed direction and went for the right-hand one. He moved and cannoned into the middle one who was thrown off balance. Before he made up his mind which way to run, I grabbed him by the lower jaw. My thumb was in his mouth, just behind the sharp incisor teeth and my fingers grasped the lower jaw-bone. He struggled briefly, circling round me. He then stood quietly and sucked tentatively at my thumb as though it was a dummy. I led him to the wall, near the door, with his backside to the light, and caught and held his tail out of the way with my free hand.

The vet leant against the calf's hip, pressing him tight against the wall, while I leant against its shoulder. The antiseptic swab was used to clean the skin of the scrotum. The scalpel, with a new blade, was so sharp that the quick initial slash through the skin caused barely a tremor of reaction from the calf. The pink shiny testicle with its fine network of bluish veins, dropped down; it was grasped and pulled firmly backwards until the connecting cord and artery ruptured. The calf grunted once and a few drops of blood stained the straw and splashed on his yellow hooves. The vet lobbed the testicle out over the half door of the loose-box where it was caught expertly by Sport. He had noted the arrival of the vet's car. He lifted one eyelid and saw that Gyp was apparently still dozing in the dust. Nonchalantly, he stood up, pottered to a corner of a rick and damped down a small area of dust. He then continued round the corner and out of Gyp's sight. His pace then became brisk and businesslike until he reached the loose-box. This was not the first time he had seen the vet go into the calves' box and he knew exactly where to sit and wait outside.

When all three had been caught and castrated, I collected a bucket of warm water, a piece of soap and a towel from the farmhouse kitchen. I stood and watched as he cleaned and dried the scalpel. The boot of his car looked like a chemist's shop and I was fascinated by the array of shining instruments laid out on a tray.

When I returned to my dust heap it had grown considerably, and the monotony of my task allowed me plenty of time to think. I thought that I'd like to be a veterinary surgeon.

CHAPTER THREE

THE BURNING COW

THE next time the vet called, the tempo of farm life had slowed down. Harvest and threshing were over and we were engaged in the pleasant task of cider making. Every year we made enough for the house and for the men to fill their three-pint wooden firkins, which was their daily ration. Boys like me were only allowed two pints.

Outside the wall of the barn which housed the cider press, Prince, an elderly grey gelding, walked round and round in a well-worn circle. His lightweight harness was attached to a pole. He supplied the power which crushed the apples. These were collected from the orchard, from the branches and the ground underneath the old, tilted, lichen-covered trees. Some were good, many partly eaten by wasps and bruised by their fall. They were all tipped into the hopper of the crushing machine.

The base of the press was a four-foot square of thick oak planks, caulked with clay. A two-inch rim contained the apple juice and a slight fall and a shallow gulley led the juice into a stone cistern below.

Chickens roosted overhead. Before cider-making could begin we had to use a shovel and then a hard bass broom to clean the base. We first laid down a bed of oat straw, and on top of this, a six-inch layer of crushed apples. Round the edge the oat straw was folded up and over, more straw added and then another layer of crushed apples. The straw and apple sandwich was built up to a height of three feet.

A wooden screw, hand-carved many generations ago and eight inches in diameter, was operated by a short wooden handle. The gentle pressure caused a little juice to flow out of the pile. Mixed with short pieces of straw and chicken droppings, it flowed into the stone cistern. A longer lever operated by two men increased the flow to a clear golden stream. I was allowed to sample this freely. It tasted like nectar and it didn't occur to me to think why nobody else was indulging in this delight. I drank over half a pint. In the small hours of the following morning, I found out why. Hurrying from my bed to the bathroom, at a crouching, anxious trot down a long corridor, I had the sensation of having drunk half a pint of castor oil. The next morning, the farm workmen enquired whether I had had a good night's sleep.

When no more juice flowed, the screw was wound back. A hay-cutting knife, with a two-foot long broad blade, was used to trim round the edges of the flattened heap. The cuttings were heaped on top and the new pile compressed again. The dry cube of straw and pith was thrown out into the yard for the benefit of the chickens, and a new pile created.

The stone cistern was baled out with buckets. They were carried in pairs with a wooden yoke to the long low cellar. A dozen hogs-heads, sixty-gallon wooden barrels, resting on heavy timbers lined one wall. Four tuns, each holding one hundred and twenty gallons, stood against the other wall.

Alternate barrels were filled and left open to 'work'. When the initial fermentation, aided by the chicken dung and bits of rotten apple, had subsided, the clear liquid was 'racked off' and transferred to the neighbouring empty barrel.

I was crossing the farmyard with the smooth wooden yoke on my shoulders supporting the two large buckets of apple juice, when the vet's car drove up and and stopped close to me. He poked his sandy head out of the window and creased the corners of his blue eyes.

'You'd make a good milk-maid. I've come to look at a sick sow. Do you know what the trouble is?'

I eased the buckets on to the ground and shed my yoke.

'I didn't know they'd called for you. We'd better go up to the house and see uncle.'

The sow had farrowed three days ago. Eighteen piglets, fourteen of them alive, but two of them runts. The first two days all was well. Now, this morning, her udders had gone hard and she was not giving enough milk to keep her piglets happy. She hadn't cleared up her food and my uncle felt that if something wasn't done she'd lose the lot.

I stood by obediently while my uncle briefed the vet. He then spoke to me.

'Take him down to the piggery and help him if necessary. And be careful how you handle her. 'Er's a proper heller.'

I led the way to the piggery. The farrowing pens were in a converted stable. Each of the six stalls had strong four-inch square oak beams fastened across the back pillars. They made six large, comfortable and draught-free pens.

The vet put his case on the floor, took out his thermometer and shook it. The sow eyed us suspiciously and gave a warning grunt—entirely different in tone from her 'piglet talk' grunts. I stayed outside while the vet climbed over the barrier, thermometer at the ready. He had one hand on her tail, when she shook herself free of her suckling offspring. For her size she had remarkable agility. She swung herself round, scattering squealing piglets, and charged at him. Just ahead of her, he vaulted the barrier. She bit at his heel and made firm contact with the old oak beam. As she closed her jaws, she twisted her head and there was a sharp crack as one of her long, offensive, canine teeth snapped off. Later on, using a chisel, we extracted half an inch of sharp tooth from the iron-hard oak.

Two farm hands were called for and, using a door as a barrier, we forced her up to the end of the stall, allowing her piglets to escape under it, to save them from being trampled. The vet leant over the door, inserted the thermometer into her rectum and waited an anxious minute. Her temperature was three degrees above normal—some of the rise, no doubt, caused by her excitement. I watched him fill a large syringe. Once more he leant over the door, stuck it into her ample rump and swiftly pushed home the plunger. She let out a high-pitched squeal of indignation and shot forward into the corner on her knees. She was too late. The syringe with bent needle attached had already been withdrawn. We retreated behind our barrier and left her grumbling to herself and her piglets.

I returned to the farmyard, to my yoke and buckets of cider.

24

One had been tipped over. The other was upright but almost empty. Daisy, a contented cow, watched me pick up the buckets and licked her lips complacently. She was the house cow, who supplied us with our daily milk, cream and butter. Having calved three months ago, she was at peak production. She was 'on bulling' and instead of being sent out to graze with the rest of the cows, she had been kept back to go to the bull. I surreptitiously emptied the dregs which Daisy had left and returned to the cider house, hoping that nobody had noticed.

The vet called again next morning. Daisy had dropped from her usual two-gallon morning yield to a mere half-gallon. She didn't appear to be very sick but the wall at the back of her stall where she had been tied up for the night was liberally plastered with very liquid dung. The passage behind her stall was five feet wide and the dung level on the wall was no more than six inches below the level of her tail.

The vet examined her carefully but was unable to form any definite opinion as to the cause of the sudden onset and exceptional severity of the diarrhoea.

After lunch, I harnessed up Prince, got into the trap and drove to town. I had to stop at the blacksmith's to collect some spare parts for a plough. I then drove on to the vet's surgery.

His dispensary was lined with large dusty bottles and jars with ornate gilt lettering in abbreviated Latin. An intriguing smell of aromatic oils, fenugreek and turpentine filled the room.

'You've come for the "jollop" for your uncle's cow?' he asked, upending a bottle and dipping the cork and neck of it in a bowl of red sealing wax which bubbled over a small spirit lamp. He reached for a wine bottle which was filled with a brown liquid with a heavy white deposit.

'Shake it well and give her two wine glasses of it in a pint of water. Drench her every four hours.'

'What do I drench her with? Cold water?' His small blue eyes watched me with suspicion.

'Don't you know how to drench a cow?' I shook my head. He continued to eye me with suspicion.

25

'If you really don't know,' he answered pedantically, 'it is the term used for administering a draught of liquid medicine to an animal, by pouring it down its throat. Whereas, "balling" an animal, such as a horse, is the term used for the oral administration of a large pill or bolus. It does not refer to its testicles.'

I took the bottle and stood watching him, hesitantly.

'If my uncle will let me, could I go around with you on your visits?'

He left me standing, clutching the bottle of medicine, while he carefully arranged the lines of red-capped bottles.

'If you really want to be a vet, you'd be starting at the wrong end by coming around with me and watching me work. You've got five or six years studying at college first. Some of it dull stuff like physics and chemistry. If you spend too much time with me or any other vet, seeing the interesting side of things, you'll find it very difficult to knuckle down to the book-work. The time to start getting interested in the practical side of things is after your third year at college. During your first three years, get to know how healthy animals behave, how they're fed and cared for. You'll then be in a better position to judge how sick they are, when you're called in to attend them.'

Disappointed, I turned to walk out. He called me back.

'If your uncle can spare you, you could come with me for a week or two. That wouldn't do any harm and you might find that being a vet wasn't as intriguing as you thought. It can be pretty unpleasant some of the time and there's quite a bit of uninteresting routine. It's also dirty and can be dangerous, as you saw yesterday morning.'

Filled with enthusiasm, I was prepared to accept all the drawbacks. I told him that I'd ask my uncle as soon as I got back. If he said 'yes' I could start after the weekend.

Prince may have been an old grey gelding but he took me back at a spanking trot and at times almost broke into a canter. I liked to think that my hands, light and gay on the reins had infected him with some of my elation but it may have been that he knew it was past his feed time and that we were headed homewards.

I spent the first hour of Monday morning bending over a tub of hot soapy water. A pile of assorted bottles, which had been picked up on previous visits to farms, had to be cleaned, the old labels and dust removed from the outside and the sticky dregs from the inside. The vet had a theory that everything came in useful, given time. One end of a shed was filled with a shelving pile, mainly of old bottles but leavened with other bric-à-brac. A cow horn, a broken bicycle pump, an old and empty wireless cabinet and a horse's hoof with shoe attached peeped out from the dusty heap—useful for what? I wondered gloomily.

Later, I loaded two wooden boxes containing bottles of medicine and injections on to the back seat of his car and waited as he gave his wife a list of the farms he was visiting. If an emergency call came in while we were out, she would have a rough idea where to get hold of us.

Most of the farms we visited were small. Usually run by the farmer and his wife, working eighteen hours a day, seven days a week. Occasionally, a son or a paid hand swelled the labour force to three. Much of the land in that part of Devon was poor, barren moorland, with outcrops of rock and ever-encroaching bracken.

The farm buildings, in keeping with the quality of the land, were ramshackle, badly ventilated and ill-lit. The calves and other young stock reared in this dismal environment started life with a considerable disadvantage. They had little resistance to the infections which flourished in the mounting piles of manure, both inside and outside their hovels. Their drinking water was drawn from the picturesque old-world type farm pond, with its attendant ducks. A small stream trickled into the pond at one side. Drainage from the cowpen and yard oozed in from the other side.

Yearling and two-year-old Devon steers were branded, and turned out on the moorland in the spring to fend for themselves. A token amount of straw or poor quality hay was fed to them to entice them to stay within reasonable limits of the home farm. Rounded up in the autumn, they were brought

27

back to the farm and yarded for the winter. Usually they were suffering from malnutrition and coughing badly from husk or lung-worm infestation. The adult worms lived in the lungs and the thousands of eggs they laid were coughed up, swallowed and the larvae passed out on to the grass in the dung. The infected grass was then eaten.

Steers that were well fed and in good condition could withstand the infection and were not badly affected. The others would develop pneumonia and die.

At that time in the 1930s the current remedy was to inject a mixture of chloroform and turpentine into the animal's trachea or windpipe. It is doubtful whether the treatment did any good at all. Any suggestion to the farmer that the injection was not really necessary was ill-received. His father and his grandfather had always had them injected, so it must be right. If you weren't prepared to do it, then he'd get someone who would, but the instructions to keep the animal housed, warm and well fed, were usually obeyed and were of considerable benefit.

The steers were wild. They had been loose on the moor all summer and resented the sight and touch of humans. They milled round and round the farmyard and they had too much space and freedom of movement for us to be able to catch them. They were driven into a shed. In the restricted space, they could be roped and drawn up, fighting every inch, to an iron ring set in the wall.

After a long dry summer on the moor, their hooves were as hard as flints and their edges as sharp. Each steer, having been injected, was freed and turned out into the yard. Only two were left and they had more space in which to manoeuvre. The casual farm-hand cast the noose of the rope expertly over the horns of one of them and hung back to take the strain. As the steer swung away from him, the slack of the rope flapped against its thigh. It lashed out backwards. The speed of the kick made the hoof a blur. It caught him between the legs and sliced through his breeches like a carving knife. The man grunted, doubled up and clutched at his crotch with both hands. We helped him to hobble outside. He half straightened up, took one hand away and looked at it. It was covered with blood and he fainted.

We rolled him on to his back and inspected the damage. The hoof had cut through the skin of his scrotum just as cleanly as it had cut through his breeches. One pink and shiny testicle lay in a small pool of congealing blood. The vet soaked a swab of cotton-wool in antiseptic, cleaned away the blood and dirt and pushed the testicle back where it belonged. Not having any needle or sutures with him, he closed the split in the scrotum with a safety-pin borrowed from the farmer's wife. With the insertion of the pin the farm-hand regained consciousness, tried to lift his head and looked blearily around.

'What happened?' he enquired.

'Nothing much,' said the vet. 'You've just dropped a bollock!'

We helped him to the car and drove him to the nearest hospital for some professional needlework.

The two steers were left un-injected. They fared as well as the others in the bunch and the farmer began to think that maybe his father and grandfather had been mistaken.

After a week of bottle-washing for the vet, I graduated to filling and labelling. The potent brew contained in the bottles with the red sealing-wax was, according to the extensive legend carried in fine print on the label, a cure for everything from indigestion to retained after-birth.

Some time later, I had the temerity to question its efficiency against such a wide range of disorders. I half expected to have my ears pinned back for being insolent, but he answered with a chuckle.

'You ought to have realised by now that many of my farming clients are primitive and bigoted in their outlook. The red-sealing-wax, like the gold foil on a bottle of champagne, is impressive. The contents have a pungent odour. They look dark and strong and the farmer is convinced that they will do his cow a "power of good". If I didn't sell him this quack remedy, he'd go and buy some obnoxious patent medicine in the market. As it is I know my stuff won't do his cow any harm and it'll give him time to make up his mind to call me in.

If it isn't in a fancy bottle with a bit of ether in it to make it go "pop" when he pulled out the cork, then it's got to have plenty of chalk or kaolin to give it a heavy deposit. He gains satisfaction from having to shake the bottle. He's convinced that if there's plenty of "body" in the medicine, it must be good.'

In that part of the country, with its peasant farming community, the status of a veterinary surgeon was judged by his ability to convince the owner, rather than by the successful treatment of the cow.

Life, on the whole, in this rural community was leisurely and unhurried. Its even tenure was broken one morning and my bottle-washing abruptly interrupted.

The vet came out of the surgery at an agile trot, urgently calling to me to get into the car. He had the engine started before I was seated.

'Sandford at Whiddon Down has got a blown cow,' he explained. 'The last one died. I was five minutes too late.'

'What's a blown cow?' I asked.

'Cows are ruminants like sheep and goats. They eat grass which passes into their rumen. It's not the true stomach but more of a storage space. It holds about forty gallons. Bacterial fermentation of the grass, which is the initial stage in its digestion, takes place in the rumen. If the grass is too lush or if there's a lot of clover in it, it forms into a soggy mass and the gas formed by the fermentation can't escape to be belched up. The rumen gets distended like a balloon. Eventually the pressure is so great that it forces it against the diaphragm and stops the cow from breathing.'

'How do you treat it?' I asked, bracing myself nervously against the dashboard as he swung the car along the winding road.

'In the early stages, an injection usually works. If the pressure is too great, the cow will die before the injection has time to work, so one has to release the pressure by puncturing the rumen.'

He reached into the glove pocket and produced an instrument which looked like a dagger. The blade was sheathed with a tight fitting, stainless steel tube.

'This is called a "trocar-and-canula". Have a look.' He dropped it on to my lap. The tyres squealed as he braked and turned off the road and into the farmyard.

The cow was lying on her side, legs stiffly extended. She appeared to be dead. He stopped the car a few feet from her, grabbed the instrument, jumped out of the car without waiting to change into his boots and squelched across the yard. He paused for a moment, looking down at her. She was still alive, but her breathing was imperceptible and her tongue, fully protruded, was a cyanotic dark blue. He stepped over her tail and using both hands, stuck the sharp trocar-and-canula through her distended flank and up to its hilt, immediately behind her ribs and below her lumbar vertebrae. He pulled out the dagger part or trocar leaving the hollow canula in position. An explosive hiss of gas and flecks of greenish grass tinged froth shot out. He stood and watched it for a few moments as the pressure subsided from its near fatal level. He then took a box of matches from his pocket, looked at me and winked.

Striking one match, he held it over the opening of the canula. A nine inch shaft of blue flame burned and flickered like a bunsen-burner from the end of the canula. The farmer and his two sons watched, open-mouthed. The gas produced by the fermentation in the cow's rumen was almost pure methane: the marsh-gas which produces the will-o'-the-wisp, and 'firedamp' which kills miners and their canaries.

As the pressure reduced, the cow's breathing became deeper and steadier. Her tongue lost its lethal blue colour and she retracted it into her mouth.

We tucked her feet under her and rolled her up on to her brisket. She struggled to her feet and walked slowly across the yard, hissing quietly through her canula.

The vet collected a bottle of medicine and a small metal funnel from the car. He fitted the nozzle of the funnel into the opening of the canula and poured the contents of the bottle straight into her rumen.

'It's easier than pouring it down her neck,' he commented to the farmer. 'In case she blows up again, I'll leave this tube in her until tomorrow. If you keep her in and give her some

31

roughage like a bit of straw or old hay, she'll be all right. I'll call tomorrow and take the tube out.'

'That was quite spectacular, wasn't it?' he remarked, as we drove back to the surgery. 'It'll give him something to talk about in the pub tonight. He's got a live cow, but she won't be so good for milking now.'

'Why not?' I asked.

'Having had that dirty great trocar stuck into her guts, she's bound to get a localised area of peritonitis or infection and inflammation. There'll be adhesions around that area which will affect the normal movements of her rumen and her digestion will be impaired.'

'Why did you set light to the gas?' I asked.

'It wasn't entirely for your benefit. As you saw, it impressed the farmer considerably. He thinks I'm a magician. It'll take his mind off the fact that she doesn't thrive so well and her milk yield's down.'

CHAPTER FOUR

CAMELS AND MULES

MY uncle's vet had been right. After the interesting practical work it was something of a let-down to have to concentrate on dull theory.

However, after five years' gestation, the parent body of the Veterinary College severed my umbilical cord and extruded me into the jealous world of professional men. A few weeks later, still wet behind the ears, I stood irresolutely outside a well-known outfitters in London, a full fledged first lieutenant in the Royal Army Veterinary Corps. I regretted having arranged to meet my parents outside the shop, the dim recesses of a café would have been better. I stood still, ramrod stiff, looking straight ahead through slightly narrowed eyes. An elderly lady chided me gently for failing to hold open the shop door. Another demanded that I whistle up a taxi. I was never able to produce a satisfactory whistle by inserting two fingers into my mouth. The result was too low-pitched, did not carry and I tended to dribble. The arrival of my parents saved me from further humiliation. Although my behaviour was unbecoming an officer and a gentleman, I left the elderly lady to call her own taxi. . . .

Warm air, carrying an unusual foreign smell—not unlike well-rotted pig manure, yet not unpleasant to a countryman—came through the port hole. The distant view of Port Said was of gracious, curving palm trees and stark square buildings glaring in the hot morning sun.

The town of Port Said was less attractive at close quarters, as we marched, three officers and thirty other Ranks of the RAVC draft to the railway station. The Other Ranks had been, in civilian life, associated with horses—stable lads, hunt servants, farriers and grooms. Discipline, in terms of Army bull-shit, was nil. Affection, under the common bond of animal sense, was high.

Under a still hotter sun, the train dragged us across the arid undulating wastes of the Sinai Desert. We stopped at Gaza, saw our first camel. Camels were not included in the curriculum at the Veterinary College. I was ignorant of their habits and general husbandry. I knew that the Middle Eastern version had one hump and that it was a ruminant like the cow and sheep. I had been told that it was possible to get venereal disease from the bite of a Camel.

I started to learn.

My failures were not buried but provided food for a small pack of foxhounds which were used for hunting jackal and the occasional Palestine fox. Some also, I suspect, found their way into various restaurants in Jaffa. During my first few months the hounds fed well. I was alarmed, and concern was expressed that the supply of camels would run out before I gained the knowledge and ability to be of any assistance to the survivors.

Bacterial examination of the mouth revealed a germ which appeared, under the microscope, to be similar to the causal organism of syphilis. It was in fact a distant but harmless relative, which exploded the VD myth.

Nobody had told me that, in common with the elephant, but unlike all other mammals the male and not the female came into season. During this time, which was called, appropriately enough, 'must', the male camel became considerably worse tempered. It was hazardous to try and approach or handle them and I was nearly decapitated by a vicious, swinging kick from a long and powerful hind leg. Another of its less attractive habits when in 'must' was the extrusion of a large, pink and wobbly balloon, not unlike 'bubble gum', from its mouth. It achieved this by blowing a distended soft-palate forward through its lips accompanied by the sound of an old man clearing his throat. Under normal conditions, a similar sound directed at a camel would induce it to kneel down, a necessary procedure before fitting a saddle. A kneeling camel can't kick, and it was safer to treat them in this position. Having an attack of catarrh was a considerable asset in issuing the word of command and obtaining the co-operation of the camel.

There was only one Army mule at Gaza. It received far more than its fair share of veterinary attention. Every Saturday, I felt it was my duty to drive down from Tel Aviv and examine it to see that all was well. Its duties were light, working two hours a day, drawing a small water-cart which supplied a NAAFI restaurant overlooking a vast expanse of sandy beach. Having finished my work, I was then able to swim and enjoy the restaurant facilities, which were limited to beer and egg and chips.

Driving south from Gaza over mile after mile of black tarmac road, snaking across a parched, yellow land, I reached Rafah, and continued on towards El Arish, an Arab village lying on the coast at the south-east corner of the Mediterranean. Progress on this section was slower. Sand drifted continually across the road surface. Any small or large obstruction, such as a large stone or petrol drum, on the windward side of the road, interrupted the smooth passage of the swirling sand and a sand-dune was born in its shadow. The smaller drifts, where they crossed the road, could be negotiated by reducing speed and bumping over them. Larger ones had to be cleared by spade work. At a dip in the road, I mistook a large dune for a small one, attempted to drive over it and became stuck up to the axle in hot shifting sand. Resting on my shovel, I surveyed the lonely emptiness. The faint hiss of sand on sand, accentuated the silence of the landscape. To the south, the road flickered and melted into an uncertain horizon.

To the north, the mirage was broken by a column of dust which I hoped marked the passage of a car, but could have been the path of a small whirlwind or dust-devil spinning drunkenly across the barren surface. As it approached, I made out the black beetle shape of a car leading its own dust cloud. A dented Ford Pilot saloon stopped on the clear road behind my car. Eighteen Arabs got out of it. I was surrounded by a sympathetic crowd of fellow travellers. The tenacious sand was defeated by the eighteen Arab-power team and I continued the journey to El Arish with the comforting knowledge that they were behind me.

The village, with its backdrop of tall date palms was typical of many and probably looked the same in Biblical times. Square box houses, 'muttee' walls constructed, as in parts of Devon, with sand, clay and straw, some their natural colour, others with peeling whitewash. They crowded on to narrow alley-ways which barely gave room for two camels to pass. I stopped my car to wave my thanks to my followers. They also stopped. A crowd of almost menacing proportions surged around my car. They insisted that I got out and accept the hospitality of El Arish. I was escorted through a narrow doorway at the end of a claustrophobic passage and found myself in a pleasant open courtyard. We sat shaded by a canvas awning, recently acquired from the British Army judging by the broad arrow and WD sign. Zibib, a local Pastis, fiercely alcoholic and strongly flavoured with aniseed, was served in small glasses, also of Army origin.

Many drinks later I weaved my way back to the car. I had been treated very reasonably; only the spare wheel, jack and tool kit, had been removed. They had left me all four wheels and the mirror.

The enclosing walls of the Governor's residence were indistinguishable from all the other walls in El Arish—peeling plaster and limewash. The large wooden gates, also in need of a coat of paint, were opened for me and I drove into a typical English garden. A trim, close-mown croquet lawn, herbaceous borders and beds of roses. A swimming pool and tennis court added to the air of quiet opulence.

The Governor's three dogs, a mixed bunch, who were the excuse, if not the sole purpose of my visit, bounded joyfully across the lawn to meet me. They did not know that I was a vet. On my second week-end visit, their joyous bounding stopped when they recognised the car. Their gait became stiff-legged and their hackles rose. They circled warily, minds ill at ease, bodies taut, around the car as though it were a canine intruder, trespassing on their private domain. The two dogs indicated their contempt on all four tyres, while the bitch looked on approvingly. They spoilt the aggressive effect by breaking into a trot halfway back across the lawn, which degenerated into a tail-down gallop as they jostled each other for first place up the verandah steps, and the imaginary security of the house.

After the second visit, either by extra-sensory perception or by the sound of the engine, they recognised my arrival and preferred to remain under the Governor's bed.

They had all been rescued as puppies from the streets of the village. Being ignorant of what their fate would have been, they showed no gratitude for having been rescued. The comfort of their surroundings and the regular meals were accepted automatically. They did not appreciate the veterinary attention. They took it as a personal insult that I should want to peer into their ears and examine their eyes and teeth. Having their temperatures taken was the last straw. They considered it a diabolical liberty that this dreadful man in khaki with his nasty little black bag should carry out this affront upon their person.

Having completed my examination, removed a few ticks and with further resentment on their part, clipped their toe-nails, I sat down with a large gin and tonic to talk with their owners. Sensing their ordeal was over, they tore round and round the room in small circles, out across the verandah, down the steps and round the lawn. Seeing my car parked on the drive, they stopped short in their tracks and approached it haughtily. They sniffed at the doors, rechristened the tyres and with a show of bravado, scratched back the gravel with short, powerful kicks of their hind legs. With renewed confidence, they trotted back to the house, slumped down on the carpet and eyed me speculatively, keeping one eye on the door.

Later, I stood up to go to my quarters to bath and change for dinner. They raised themselves expectantly on to their fore-paws and eyed me again. I was followed out of the room and along the verandah. When they saw that I was not going towards my car, they turned back, their hopes dashed.

Dinner was an elegant, black-tie, occasion. Standing in attentive silence behind each diner was a tall black Sudanese waiter, clad in a spotless white galabeah, with a broad red

37

cummerbund to match his tarbush. Sitting near my feet, under the table, were all three hairy little mongrels. They had apparently decided to call a truce during meal-times.

One cold nose tentatively touched my bare ankle—I'd forgotten to bring my black socks. The other leg was subjected to gentle but insistent pressure from a paw with curved toe-nails. It was difficult to pass clear consommé surreptitiously under the table, especially under the eye of the Sudanese waiter. Small pieces of fish established the fact that I was prepared to co-operate in observing the truce, but the paw and nose pressure continued until the end of the entrée.

The following morning all this cupboard love was forgotten. They perhaps resented the fact that I had taken breakfast in my room and denied them the chance of cementing our friendship. They eyed me with distrust when I emerged. A vet was a vet, whether in uniform or mufti, and was not to be trusted except when feeding. They followed me at a respectably safe distance until I left the premises to explore the surrounding village.

I was welcomed, with some reservation, by two of the Arabs who had entertained me the day before. I felt it would have been churlish to have mentioned the loss of the spare tyre and tool kit from my car. They could have taken much more, WD property was fair game for them. It was not my personal property, hence they were not breaking their time-honoured code of offering shelter and protection to a traveller. Seeing that I was not in uniform and was not going to complain about the loss of the tit-bits from my car, they decided to continue our friendship with a conducted tour of El Arish.

The market-place was an open square on the outskirts of the village. Heaps of dusty straw marked the areas where the meagre crops were threshed by the circling, plodding hooves of a muzzled mule. Little else but water melons, goats and camels were offered for sale or barter.

In one corner of the arena was a small crowd of Arabs, their camels kneeling by them or standing, halter-held, watching the proceedings with supercilious expressions. The centre of attraction was an elderly gentleman in a dirty striped galabeah, squatting on the floor. Purple suspenders peeped coyly from under the hem. His dirty toes scuffed absentmindedly in the dust. A small beaten brass and enamel goblet stood on a mat in front of him. He picked it up, sipped the contents, savoured them on his tongue, and replaced the utensil. The one who had provided the goblet passed him a handful of piastres which he tucked carefully out of sight in the folds of his galabeah. He then looked at the man and shook his head. This ceremony was repeated several times, occasionally the answer was 'yes'.

When no more goblets were forthcoming, I was taken over and introduced to him. He looked at me with his one good eye, which emanated distrust and hostility. Not wishing to continue the interview, I turned and left. My companions were most apologetic. They excused his behaviour as being due to professional jealousy. Apparently he suspected that I might try to usurp his position as the accepted diagnoser of pregnancy in camels. A pregnant camel secretes a higher quantity of sugar in her urine than a non-pregnant camel. If one has a sufficiently delicate palate it is possible to distinguish the difference and one's services are in constant demand.

Shortly after my week-end at El Arish, a RAF officer asked me to examine his dog. It was dribbling profusely and unable to close its jaws. He had already diagnosed the cause as being due to a bone stuck in its throat. He wanted me to remove it. Inexperienced, brash and anxious to please, I stroked the dog on the head and plunged my hand into its mouth. There was no bone or any other form of obstruction in its mouth or throat. A small cold thread of fear crept up my back and prickled the short hairs on the nape of my neck. This dog was suffering from rabies. Not the more usual violent form, where they rush about biting at everyone and everything, but the less common dumb rabies. It was just as infectious as the common form and equally lethal to humans if untreated.

The dog was kept under observation for five days. When, according to the normal pattern of the disease it died, I removed the head and took it to a nearby research institute which had the facilities for diagnosing rabies. The result was positive. While smarting under the indignity of having fifteen daily injections, I was able to reflect on my own stupidity.

My hunting, polo-playing and the pleasant week-ends at El Arish were interrupted by a transfer to Syria and mules.

I knew as much about mules as I did camels, when I first started. Anatomically, I knew that they closely resembled horses. Being recently qualified, all the bits and pieces that went to make up a horse were fresh in my mind. Mentally, as with most hybrids, they are far superior to the horse. Appreciated and handled with respect, they are more co-operative than the majority of horses. If treated badly, they can and will retaliate effectively. When subjected to mortar and shell-fire, unlike horses, they did not panic. In mountainous country and difficult terrain, if given their heads and allowed time to think, they would descend slopes that a horse or pack pony would look at, rear up on its hind legs, and bolt off, spreading panic among the followers. The mule would survey the scene, then ease his hind legs forward until they were level with his front hooves. Sitting down like a dog, all four feet splayed out in front and acting as brakes, he would slide down on his bottom. He usually arrived with his load intact and appeared to enjoy the experience.

If caught up in barbed wire, a horse would kick himself to ribbons in his efforts to escape. A mule had the sense to stand still, and allow you to crawl around his legs, clipping the wire away. Once he was free and quite certain that he was not going to hurt himself, he might then offer you a parting kick.

His digestion was stronger than a horse. He could cope with a variety of food, including his neighbour's horse-rug and bits of harness. He seldom got digestive upsets or colic. His feet, though the hooves were small and unattractive to any self-respecting farrier, were sound and tough. Lameness, common in horses, was almost unknown in mules even though they frequently worked unshod.

His one weak point was the skin of his back. Unless his harness fitted perfectly and his load was carefully balanced, deep-seated sores developed. These sores took months to heal and having healed the resulting scar tissue would break down

40

again after a few weeks' work.

Contrary to popular belief, mules are sexually normal, except that they are infertile. They have all the right or wrong instincts, depending on one's point of view. On one occasion I was riding an in-season mare through a town when we were chased by an enthusiastic uncastrated male mule. He was running under a considerable handicap as he was harnessed to a milk float. He made a brave effort and the noise was spectacular. We eluded him by turning into a narrow alleyway which was not wide enough to accommodate his float.

The mule is the end of a short line of two, a male or jack donkey and a female horse or mare. Two mules, though willing and able to mate, produce no offspring. A pony stallion mated to a female donkey produces a jennet; these are also infertile and of little commercial value as they are small in stature compared with mules. Some mules, depending on the size of their dam, the mare, can be as big as carthorses and stronger.

The British Army owes a considerate debt of gratitude to the mule. The ordinary British soldier, when informed that they were to become muleteers, viewed the matter in a different light. But having accepted and, in most cases, been accepted by their charges, they changed their opinion. The British soldier and the mule were compatible and at times inseparable. They had a similar sense of humour, accentuated by adversity. They were equally tough, resilient and adaptable. In the mountains of Italy and the jungles of Burma, pack mules were indispensable. Hundreds of them were 'de-voiced' by having, under suitable anaesthesia, their vocal cords removed. A silent mule, unable to whinny or bray, was a necessity when operating with the long-range penetration groups. They were flown in by Dakota aircraft and few returned.

With the end of the fighting in Italy, I was taken off mules and moved to Egypt.

I had a mixed practice, stretching from Port Said to Suez, down the 100-mile length of the Canal. My patients were horses, guard-dogs and a herd of water buffalo.

The horses had been shipped out to the Middle East as a

Cavalry Division. On mechanisation of the Division, other work had to be found for the horses. Some were used by the Mounted Military Police, the majority ended their useful lives pulling wagons round the docks and large storage depots. The senior farrier at Suez was shoeing the very same horses that he had shod some years before in Knightsbridge Barracks.

The Military Police Dogs were boxers, alsatians and a few dobermans. We waged a perpetual battle against ticks. The handler would remove fifty or more ticks from his dog one evening, to find a similar number on the following evening. They were responsible for carrying a malaria-like disease called biliary or tick fever—a serious disease and often fatal. Taking a dog's temperature was a difficult and often inaccurate task. The shade temperature was over 110 and one's thermometer, unused, registered this figure and could not be shaken down. It was necessary to cool it in ice, if available, then shake it down and use it very quickly. On removal from the dog's rectum, the column of mercury rose relentlessly and rapidly to the 110 mark again. It had to be checked immediately or read *in situ*, an undignified procedure.

After my first encounter with the water buffaloes, over a hundred of them, I left them alone with their Arab herdboys. I think that they resent all Europeans; they certainly resented me. There being some resemblance to a cow, I thought I could handle them in the same way. The head is large and heavy, the neck muscles extremely powerful and the horns like two battering rams. To restrain a cow, one grasps it by the nostrils. The same procedure infuriates a water buffalo. A mighty sideswipe lifted me off my feet and draped me over the back of her neighbour, who shrugged me off and tried to trample me. I was dragged clear by two of the herdboys, who appeared to find the incident very amusing.

Shortly after this humiliating episode, the war being over, the Army felt that they could dispense with my services and I returned to England, civilian life and the comparative security of country practice.

CHAPTER FIVE

A COW AND A TENNIS-BALL

ON graduating, I had been presented with an impressive scroll, now demurely framed black, which proclaimed to all who chose to read it that I was qualified to practise the Art and Science of Veterinary Medicine.

After five years at the Veterinary College, I was more than confident that I had mastered the Science. I was also aware of the Art. Now, after three years of drinking gin and playing polo, I was less confident about the Science and was beginning to entertain doubts about the Art.

My framed diploma hung on the wall behind the door in the waiting-room and was unfortunately only visible when there were no clients waiting and the door was shut. During my first few weeks as an assistant in the practice, I frequently went into the waiting-room, ostensibly to arrange the meagre selection of outdated magazines. I was always careful to shut the door and having completed my self-appointed task, would spend long moments looking with pride at the fruit of my five years' endeavour. Hanging over the dismal empty fireplace which was the focal point of the room, were the similarly framed documents of my employers—Bill, the principal of the practice and his junior partner, Mike. These appeared to carry more authority, as their frames lacked the new high lustre of mine and their inks had faded suitably. I had hoped, on my arrival, that they would move over and make room for me on the same wall, but it was decided that it would upset the balance.

One morning, in surgery, a client whose dog I was examining enquired solicitously as to when I hoped to qualify. Quite obviously she had not looked behind the waiting-room door. I was prepared to overlook this omission and her ignorance of my qualified status, but I resented the use of the word 'hope', implying as it did that there was some doubt as to whether I would ever actually succeed in qualifying.

From the beginning I was mainly employed on routine tasks which required little or no diagnostic skill: the preventive inoculation of flocks of sheep against dysentery and allied disorders, vaccination of pigs and TB-testing cows.

One morning when I had finished castrating a bunch of six calves on a farm, I washed my hands in a bucket of cold water and dried them on an old sack. The farmer's son, who had been helping me to catch and hold them, asked me if, as I was there, I would look at one of the heifers. I walked with him to the yard which contained the heifers. The affected one was caught, fitted with a rope halter and tied to the railings.

Some three weeks earlier, Bill, the principal of the practice, had been called in to examine her as she had a swelling on her cheek and had not been feeding as well as the others in the bunch. The swelling had been diagnosed as an abscess. It had apparently not been ready for lancing, so the hair had been close-clipped over the area and iodine painted on to the skin to accelerate its ripening. Some two weeks later, Mike, the junior partner, while visiting the farm, had been asked to re-examine the heifer as the abscess did not appear to be coming to a head. After examining the swelling which, although tense and fluctuating, was still covered with a fair thickness of skin, he decided to inject penicillin deep into its centre.

This time I was asked to look at it because there was no apparent change. I clamped a pair of 'bulldogs' into the heifer's nostrils to control the movement of her head and to occupy her mind. Having tentatively fingered the swelling, I thought that I felt it move slightly. I decided to see what it looked and felt like from the inside. I fitted a 'Drinkwater' gag between the upper and lower molar teeth on the opposite side of the mouth.

Grasping her warm rough tongue in my left hand, I eased it forward out of her mouth and slid in my right hand. I found the swelling and explored it with my fingertips. It was just as tense and fluctuating as it had felt on external examination, but it now seemed to be more clearly defined. Once more, I thought I felt it move so I grasped it as firmly as I could with forefinger and thumb and gave it a tentative pull. It definitely moved though it was still lodged between the molar teeth and the cheek. I hooked my finger more firmly round the posterior curvature of the swelling and pulled harder. It came away freely into my hand and I brought it out into the light to examine it.

The farmer's son, who had been holding on to the 'bulldogs' and peering over my shoulder at the same time, asked me what I'd found. By way of an answer I threw it at him. With a look of disgust, he ducked out of the way and let it fall in the straw. I retrieved it and held it up for him to examine, commenting that he should not have been afraid of a mere tennis-ball. On first sight it did not look much like one. It was dark grey, sodden with saliva and had one side rubbed down to the canvas by the abrasive action of the teeth. It had also been treated with iodine and injected with penicillin.

When I got back to the surgery, Bill was telling one of the surgery girls to sterilise his syringes and to make up a glucose-saline injection for a heifer that had had a rough time calving and was still shocked and unable to stand up.

He asked me how I'd got on with the calves. I told him that all had gone well. I decided that it was better to keep quiet about the tennis-ball, thinking, correctly as it happened, that my small success following the earlier mis-diagnosis might give rise to a little resentment. Secretly, I was feeling rather pleased with myself. It had helped to restore my self-esteem, which had, in the time since I qualified, taken many blows.

To counteract any tendency on my part to assume that my diagnostic skill was superior to that of my seniors, I was direc-ted to the less savoury tasks that arose, one of them being the manual removal of the cleansing or afterbirth from cows which had calved many days earlier and which by then produced a ripe and penetrating stench. The after-birth, in a cow, is normally attached by about forty buttons or cotyledons. Each one has to be carefully peeled. If any are left behind they will go even more rotten and induce a septic metritis which could prove fatal to the cow. If it didn't kill her, it could render her infertile. From the cow's point of view, the end result would be the same, since the farmer kept her for breeding and milk production. I felt that there were better ways of spending a morning than standing with one hand and an arm up to the shoulder, gently exploring the dark and slimy recesses of a cow's uterus.

It could take well over half an hour to cleanse a cow. The smell would linger on my arm for more than twenty-four hours, in spite of frequent washings in strong disinfectant.

Until she got to know me better and learned to accept the strange habits of veterinary surgeons, my landlady used to give me some very odd looks, especially at meal-times and when I warmed up at night in front of the fire. Before going off to bed, she would fiddle nervously with the ornaments on the mantel-piece, cough hesitantly and suggest that, as the water was so hot and it seemed a pity to waste it, perhaps I would like to have a bath. In time she became familiar enough to ask how I acquired the various smells and blood stains.

The de-horning of cows always produced a variety of blood-stained shirts. If nature was allowed to take her course, many a cow with a crumpled horn would suffer under a mounting crescendo of pain, as the tip of the distorted horn grew slowly yet relentlessly into her eyeball, until it destroyed the eye and even entered the skull at the back of the orbital cavity.

Twice the farmer had sawn an inch off the tip as it approached and nearly touched the eye. On the third occasion, his saw drew blood, the cow bellowed with pain and threw her head about so that it was impossible for him to continue the operation. The bony core of the horn, liberally supplied with nerves and blood vessels, was now at the very end and only protected by a thin layer of horn. The farmer gave up his attempt and came to us for advice.

I arrived at the farm, changed into my rubber thigh boots and a clean brown protective coat and went in search of the cowman. The cow was tied up by a neck chain in a loose-box and it needed only a cursory glance for me to decide that the only remedy was to remove the entire horn.

The fire in the boiler which supplied the steam to sterilise the milking equipment was unlit. An old painter's blow-lamp was unearthed, dusted off and coaxed into life with liberal applications of methylated spirit. I took two wooden-handled irons from the boot of my car. They had been designed originally for line-firing horses with sprained tendons. They were now to be used for sealing off the cut arteries after the horn had been severed. I arranged them so that the flame of the blow-lamp played on their business ends and gave the plunger of the lamp a few extra pumps for good measure. 'Bulldogs' were clamped on to the cow's nostrils, to restrain her and to give some measure of control over the movement of her head. The cowman held on to them while I clipped the hair close around the base of the horn. I swabbed the area with antiseptic and another area in the fossa or pit situated just behind the eye. Through the skin in this area, I injected local anaesthetic using a one and a half inch-long wide-bore hypodermic needle to block off the nerve supply to the horn. She flinched and twisted her head with the initial prick of the needle. Then she stayed quiet and behaved herself. I allowed five minutes for the anaesthetic to work before testing its effectiveness by pricking the skin around the base of the horn. There was one area at the back which was still sensitive and the cow reacted with a violent shaking of her head. I injected more anaesthetic, and again allowed time for it to take effect.

Using a large-bladed scalpel I cut a guide line through the skin at the base of the horn. I laid the saw edge along the cut, adjusted the angle of the blade and started sawing. She was an elderly cow and the bone was hard. It took three or four minutes of strenuous elbow-work before the horn flopped down, held only by a tongue of skin at the under edge. Blood was pumping out of numerous small arteries in gently curving arcs which varied with each pulse of the heart. It sprayed the wall and floor of the loose-box. I jammed the horn back up into position to cut down the flow and lessen the mess, while I severed the remaining flap of skin with my scalpel and called for a hot iron. Carefully, I took hold of the wooden handle, having on a previous occasion, by not paying attention, grasped the hot end. Holding it poised ready, I let the horn drop on the floor. Before I could apply the iron to seal the arteries, the cow swung her head round and a spray of hot arterial blood slashed in a bright red line across my face, the collar of my shirt and down my clean brown coat. Squinting through my right eye, as the lid and lashes of my left one were gummed up with warm and sticky clotted blood, I aimed the red-hot end of the iron at the base of the biggest artery and held it till it sizzled to a stop. I treated the remaining blood vessels in a similar fashion, then watched and waited for a few moments in case the bleeding began again. Before removing the bulldogs from her nose, I wiped the blood from around the cut area and from where it had matted the hair down her cheek. This was not primarily for aesthetic reasons but to make her less attractive to flies.

In the dairy, with a bucket of warm water and some cotton-wool, I unstuck the lashes of my eye and cleaned up the rest of my face, but could do nothing about the bright red dotted line which ran down my collar and across the front of my white shirt.

CHAPTER SIX

THE COWMAN'S POCKET

THE alarm clock interrupted my sleep at six a.m. Barely awake, I washed and shaved, dressed myself in old clothes and drank a cup of tepid coffee.

I arrived at the farm just before seven, put on my rubber thigh boots and brown overall and walked through the dairy into the milking parlour in search of the cowman. He was bending down putting the teat cluster of the milking machine on to a cow. When it was in place and the suction was drawing the milk out, he adjusted the cord over the cow's loins and turned round to look at me.

'Hello, Sid. How's it going? Ready for me?'

'Shan't be long now,' he answered. 'These are the last three. Will you wait or do you want to make a start on the calves?'

'We'll do the calves later, when the rest of the men are around to help catch and hold them. I'll fill my syringes now and then wait for you.'

When the cowman had finished, he let the cows back into the collecting yard. Then we ran the whole milking herd, one by one, through the parlour. I had to tuberculin-test each one. This involved clipping the hair off two small areas of skin on the side of the cow's neck, measuring the thickness of the skin with calipers and injecting a small amount of tuberculin into the skin in each area. The farmer came in halfway through.

'Good morning. When do you think you'll be finished with the cows?'

'At the rate we're going, we should be through by nine or quarter past,' I answered. 'It's gone very smoothly, up to now.'

'Good. The men can take their half-hour lunch break then and if you come up to the house, there'll be some breakfast for you.'

I thanked him and continued working. The last cow was driven into the parlour. Once more I clipped and measured the skin, shouted out the measurements to the cowman who was writing down all the particulars, including the cow's name and age. I used automatic syringes which delivered the correct dose, re-set themselves and only needed refilling after twenty cows. In spite of this labour-saving device, it was a tedious business. When I finally straightened up and stretched my arms, I was ready for that breakfast—102 cows, 204 injections, not counting the ones I'd missed and had had to re-inject because the cow had jerked at the wrong moment. I had been working at top speed to get through them in just over two hours and any break from the back-aching monotony would be welcome. I walked out of the milking parlour, left my syringes and other equipment in the car and took a short cut across a small meadow to the back door of the farmhouse.

It was a quiet, still morning with a hazy sun and a heavy dew. The toe-caps of my rubber boots were shining black from the wet grass and, on looking back, my footprints remained dark green on the milky background. I felt at ease and happy to be in the open air after the bustle of the cows and the clanging of the chains and tubular steel gates in the close confines of the milking parlour.

I arrived at the back door and went in unannounced, wondering why any farmhouse had a front door, as they never seemed to be used and were usually on the least accessible side of the building. I kicked off my boots in the back porch and padded across the stone flags into the kitchen. My socks, wet and sweaty from their incarceration in the rubber boots, left dark stains on the floor. The aroma of coffee, fried eggs and bacon caused my olfactory nerves to twitch with delight. The farmer's wife, large and contented, not unlike one of the cows, bustled into the kitchen as I finished washing my hands and told me to sit down and make myself comfortable. I eased myself along the bench between the wall and a well scrubbed wooden table and was presented with a heavy white plate covered with eggs, bacon and fried potatoes, followed by a large, steaming jug of coffee. She bade me, in a motherly way, eat it up and bustled out again. Having done as I was told, I was relaxing with the coffee and a cigarette when the farmer came in, carrying the morning paper and a fistful of mail. He sat down opposite to me and pointed to my plate.

'Had enough to eat?'

'Yes, thank you. Plenty and just what I needed.'

'When you've finished your coffee, we'll go and make a start on the calves while the men are bringing down the in-calf and bulling heifers. There are about a dozen calves to cut, eighteen heifer calves for Abortion vaccine and about fifteen cows for pregnancy diagnosis. You'll do all that on Monday when you come to do the reading of the test, won't you?'

I made a note on my cigarette packet.

'It'll be easier to do them on Monday. Always less of a rush then, only having to measure the swelling, if any. No clipping and injecting.'

'Good. If you're ready, we'll make a start.'

There were forty-two calves ranging from two-days to six-months old in groups of six, in small loose-boxes. The younger ones, though they tended to wriggle, were no problem. The older ones were much more lively, but I enjoyed the challenge and the exercise involved in catching them. Both the cowmen were away getting in the heifers and the men available to help were normally tractor drivers and not so accustomed to handling livestock. They tried grasping them round the neck but this amorous embrace was unsuitable for controlling 200 pounds of Friesian calf. When it came to charging round and round the loose-box, it was the calf who normally won. Their nostrils were too small to be gripped with a finger and thumb and, unlike a cow or heifer which could usually be controlled in this fashion, the calves resented it, struggled more and often threw themselves to the ground in their efforts to escape. With the experience gained from my time on the farm, I showed the men how to hold and control them effectively by grasping the lower jaw with the thumb in the side of the mouth, behind the incisor teeth. By the time we had finished testing the calves, the in-calf heifers had been rounded up, brought in and yarded.

This was one of the few farms which did not have a cattle crush or catching crate, either of which would have made life much easier and less hazardous for all concerned. With much shouting and the occasional swipe with a stick, the heifers, big two-year-old Friesians, were driven into an empty bull-pen. Being jammed in tight, they were not able to move far or fast. Neither was I nor the cowman.

We selected one near the gate, the cowman squeezed himself along one side of it until he reached its head. He put an arm over its neck and grasped its ear. At the same time, with the other hand, he grabbed hold of its nose, with his thumb in one nostril and two fingers in the other one. I worked my way up the other side, squeezing past its hot, steaming dung-covered flank. I read the number on its ear-tag, then clipped, measured and injected its neck. The cowman then let it go and by tapping it gently on the nose, drove it out backwards through the gate. We repeated the manoeuvre with the next one.

With the third one, the cowman missed the nose with his first grab, the heifer swung away from him and planted one hoof squarely on my foot. She was a ten-hundred-weight animal and it seemed to me that she was supporting most of her half-ton weight on my one foot. I let out a yell of anguish and heaved myself against the heifer's shoulder to shift her weight. The cowman, by way of sympathy, gave a hoot of coarse laughter and asked me how much she weighed. I was not at that moment amused and having freed my foot, stood muttering to myself, sweating with pain and flexing my toes inside the boot to convince myself that they weren't broken. After a few minutes, we continued until all twenty in the batch had been tested. I then limped out of the pen, lit a cigarette and waited until they brought the younger bulling heifers into the yard. There were thirty of these and a young Hereford bull who was running with them. Once more, we packed them into the pen. We caught and tested the bull first, to get him out of the way before he got upset. He was no trouble to handle once the cowman had got hold of the ring in his nose.

While we were driving the bull, who was slow and reluctant to move, out of the pen, I noticed that one of the heifers was starting to lift her tail. They were all a bit loose, having been down on a water meadow with plenty of lush grass and also because, more than likely, they were carrying a fairly heavy worm burden. The rear end of this heifer was close up to the side of the cowman. His attention being diverted towards the bull, he failed to notice the significant lifting of the tail. At the appropriate moment, I gently eased open the side pocket of the cowman's jacket which was then filled to the brim. The cowman gave the bull a friendly slap on the rump to help him out of the gate and turned back to catch one of the heifers. I stopped him and asked for a cigarette. Willingly, he plunged his hand into his jacket pocket. There was a moment's pause, a pregnant silence and a frozen look spread over his face. Slowly and carefully, he withdrew his hand, fingers stiffly extended and dripping. This time it was my turn to give the hoot of laughter. He gave me a suspicious look and attempted to retrieve his packet of cigarettes. Generously, I took out my own pack and offered him one.

The younger heifers were more flighty and difficult to catch. It was nearly noon and lunch time by the time we had finished. It was so pleasant, having the bull-pen empty and to ourselves, we leaned against the railings and smoked a cigarette each. There were now only twelve Galloway steers to be tested. They were still out grazing and we decided that they should be left until after lunch, when we were all rested and more fit to cope with them.

At one o'clock we joined the men who were waiting for us in the yard. The steers were some distance away in a field on the other side of the road. Leaving one man behind to turn them into the yard, the rest of us walked up the lane to the main road, checking that all the gates on the way were shut and securely latched. We walked two hundred yards along the main road before turning into the field. The steers were a belligerent bunch in the far corner of the field. One man was left in the road to warn traffic and to try and direct them the right way when they emerged from the gateway, another was left guarding the open gate and the rest of us, split into two groups, approached the steers from either side. The whole bunch started to move along the hedgerow to the other corner of the field. We let them go. When they reached the corner, they turned and moved down the hedge towards the gate. So far, so good. The gate had been left open but was hinged on the side from which the cattle were approaching. Three men ran across to the other side of the gateway to stop them from running past the opening and to divert them out into the road. Bunched close together, they reached the gate, flowed round it and, faced by the three men, turned into the road. Two of the bunch went the wrong side of the gate and were trapped between it and the hedge. In a panic to join the others, one of them tried to jump the gate, landed across it with a splintering of wood, struggled free and shot out into the road. The other one swung round and charged the hedge which did not give way. It then turned round and high-tailed it back up the field. Three of us followed to round it up and bring it back. Being on its own and unable to see the rest of the herd, it was thoroughly upset and was circling round, tail erect and wild eye, at the top end of the field. We tried to drive it back to the gate. It had other ideas and swung round and charged past me, lashing out with a hind leg as it did so. It missed me and the momentum of its charge carried it right through the hedge, the other side of which was a cottage garden. I scrambled after it through the ragged hole and watched it demolish a fine row of scarlet runner beans, put one foot through the glass top of a seedling frame and disappear down the side of the cottage in the direction of the front garden. I followed it and was met by an enormous bosom, above and behind which was a red and angry face. Two arms like small red hams, flecked with soap suds, were planted firmly on ample hips.

'Someone's going to have to pay for all this. Them bullicks didn't ought to be in that field. Them's as wild as 'awks and allus breaking out. Them's a proper dratted nuisance.'

I muttered an apology, dodged round the angry mountain and took the same escape route as the bullock. The neat and tidy front lawn was deeply pitted with hoof marks and a cluster of hollyhocks lay scattered and broken over the front wall. I let myself out through the front gate, shutting it carefully after me. The steer had crossed the road, cleared the hedge on the other side and was disappearing at a steady trot towards the wood at the far end of an eighteen acre field. I watched it go for a moment, then walked down the road to the top of the farm lane. The rest of the bunch of steers were moving down it towards the farm-yard and I joined the men who were driving them. Nodding in the direction of the one who had gone spare, I spoke to the under-cowman.

'That's one that's passed the test. We shan't be seeing him again today. When we've finished testing this bunch of bovine delinquents, I should turn them out in that field and he'll be able to join them when he's in a better frame of mind.'

The remaining eleven were driven into the farm-yard and eventually crowded into the bull-pen. It was out of the question to go into the pen with them and handle them as we had done with the heifers. Using a long wagon rope with a noose at one end and a knot to stop it drawing tight and choking them, we lassoed each one. Fighting all the way, they were dragged up to the bars of the gate. I stood outside the gate, and tested them in comparative safety. It was three o'clock before we finished. It had taken as long to round up and test eleven steers as it had taken to test all one hundred and two cows.

CHAPTER SEVEN

TWIN CALVES

WITH a short strident bellow, coinciding with a final heave, the calf was born. It lay, darkly damp and steaming in the soiled straw. Large long-lashed eyes blinked passively at its strange surroundings. Its bright and brand new translucent hooves threshed feebly in the air.

The telephone had rung shortly after evening surgery and I had answered it. I was on duty for night calls and I was not displeased. I felt that it was better to be out working than sitting making small-talk with my landlady.

Lower Hone Farm was only six miles away; there was an easy drive up to the dairy and a wide concrete apron in front of it. I would not have to step out of the car into six inches of ripe farmyard mud.

In addition to the luxury of the concrete, there was usually hot water available and electric light. What was more important was the cowman—intelligent, with an easy and pleasant manner. He would have kept an eye on the cow from the time that he saw she was 'springing' to calve. He would not have got in a panic and called for help prematurely. As the cow had been straining for some time, with no apparent result, he had disinfected his arm and hand and felt inside. Finding only one leg presented, he had left it alone. He had not tried to manipulate it and deliver it himself. A lesser cowman would think that to have to call in the vet on any occasion was an admission of his own inefficiency. He would spend a long time trying to calve the cow himself. By the time he was willing to admit defeat, the cow would be exhausted, bruised and dry and the calf probably dead.

I finished speaking to the farmer and put down the phone. I stood thinking for a moment. I then drove the short distance to the surgery to collect the large metal instrument box which contained all the calving equipment—ropes, hooks, wire saw and assorted knives.

On the way I decided to stop and see if Anne, the girl from New Barn Stables, was at home and ask her if she'd like to come to the farm with me.

I'd been to the stables the morning before to look at a lame horse and had been paring out the sole of one of its fore feet when I caught sight of a pair of jodhpur boots, jodhpurs and a man's white shirt. I found the hole where the nail had punctured the sole, so I let the foot go and straightened up. The occupier of the jodhpur boots was standing quietly looking at me. She was very attractive.

'You're new here. Aren't you?' was all that I could think of saying.

'Yes. I started last Monday. It's my first job.'

I bent down, picked up the foot again and started cutting away at the hoof around the site of the nail puncture. As I pared the horn down to the sensitive layer of the sole, the horse became more and more restless, feeling the increasing pressure of the hoof-knife. Every so often it tried to pull its leg and foot away from where it was clamped between my legs. Anne moved round behind me and stood at the horse's head. She talked quietly to it and smoothed her hand down its neck. I made one more cut and black pus welled up out of the hole.

'Do you want to have a look?' I said.

She left the horse's head and bent down to peer at the foot which I still held, clamped between my knees. A loose strand of her hair tickled my cheek. Looking closely, she asked, 'Why is it black?'

'I don't know. It always is black when you get a puncture wound and infection in the foot. Probably due to the sulphur content in the horn of the hoof.'

She watched while I poured iodine into the hole and packed it with cotton-wool.

'Is the boss about?'

'He took a ride out about an hour ago, but he should be back in a little while.'

57

'Tell him,' I said, 'he's got to soak this foot in salt water, night and morning for the next five days. Take out the plug of cotton-wool first of course. Bung some more iodine and a fresh lump of wool in, after he's finished soaking it. It might be a good idea to get the blacksmith to cut out a strip of metal to tuck in under the shoe. It'll help to keep the plug in and the dirt out. I'll call round in three days' time to see how it's going on. If he's not happy about it, he can give me a ring at the surgery. I'll give it an anti-tetanus injection now and leave it at that.'

She looked uncertain.

'If you would wait a little while, Captain Henry will be back and you could explain everything to him. I might not get it right if I try and tell him myself. Would you like a cup of tea or something?'

'What's the alternative?'

'Cold water.'

'I ought not to stop, but if you think he'll only be a few minutes, I'll be happy to take tea with you.'

She led the horse back to his box while I took my instrument case and syringe back to the car. By the time I got back, she was already in the tack-room, had put the kettle on for tea and was busy rinsing two chipped china mugs under a cold tap. I stood watching her. Her jodhpurs fitted almost too well, as though they had been cut for effect rather than comfort.

'What made you decide to come and work here?' I asked.

'I like working with horses. I didn't want to do anything else when I left school. I used to come here to ride before I got my own mare, then Daddy started grumbling about the cost of keeping her. Captain Henry was looking for a stable-girl and he allows me to keep my mare here provided I use her for taking out rides. I don't let anyone else ride her, except Captain Henry.'

'Does he pay you a decent wage?'

'I get five pounds a week and all Cherry's keep. It isn't very much, but I get all the riding I want and when we're not busy, I can sunbathe out at the back.'

'I must come round here when you're not busy.'

58

There was a clatter of hooves in the yard as the horses came in from the ride, accompanied by the jingling of bits and the creak of leather as they unsaddled.

Captain Henry walked briskly across the yard and into the tack room. He was a small cheerful man and carried his fifty-five years well, in spite of the worries of trying to make the stables pay with the ever-increasing costs of forage and the other overheads like vets' bills and keeping the horses properly shod.

'Hello, Anne. Any tea left? Or has the vet drunk it all? What did you find in the horse's foot? It was the foot, wasn't it? There seemed to be some heat in it last night.'

I swallowed the last of my tea, described what I'd found and explained the treatment.

'I asked him to wait for you,' explained Anne. 'I thought I might not get it right. I don't mind giving the treatment. I'd like to have been a vet myself.'

I declined the offer of a second mug of tea and drove off.

When I got back to the surgery, Bill, the senior partner was already in from his rounds.

'How did you get on with the horse at New Barn stables?'

'All right,' I answered. 'It would have been better if he'd called us in a few days earlier.'

'I expect he was hoping he wouldn't have to. He's not having an easy time up there. He sunk all his money into the stables when he retired from the army and now, with increasing costs, he's having a job to make ends meet. He owes us quite a bit, but I don't like to press him for it.'

'He's got a girl working for him now,' I pointed out. 'Quite a good-looker.'

'That will be the Bennett girl. She used to cadge rides up there before she got her own horse.'

'She said her father grumbled about the cost of keeping her horse. What does he do for a living?'

'He runs a garage and filling-station out on the road to Lower Hone Farm. They seem to be fairly comfortably off. I don't expect Captain Henry pays her much.'

*

I left the car in the forecourt of the garage and walked down a passage to the side door, feeling rather self-conscious and unsure what I was going to say. I felt like going back to the car. At that moment a middle-aged woman came round the corner from the back of the house with a very overweight dachshund at her heels. She said 'hello' and the dachshund started a high-pitched yapping bark which put an end to any further conversation. I stood with an embarrassed smile while the woman opened the door and shooed the dog inside. With sign language, she indicated that I should follow the dog. It was an undignified entrance, not at all as I had planned.

The woman shut the dog in a room and its yapping was pleasantly muffled. She came back and asked me what I wanted.

'Is Anne Bennett in?' I asked.

The woman half turned and called over her shoulder to a closed door.

'Anne. It's someone for you.'

The door opened and Anne came into the hall. She was wearing bare feet, tight-stretched blue ski pants and a sloppy white sweater.

'Hello. What are you doing here?' she asked, pleasantly.

'I was passing by and thought you might like to come along and watch me calve a cow.'

'Do what?' she queried.

'Calve a cow. She's been having a bit of trouble producing a calf. I've got to help her.'

'Do you have to be there every time a cow has a calf?'

I explained to her that they normally manage themselves, but sometimes the cowman acts as midwife. This cow had been straining for several hours and nothing had happened.

'You said you were interested in animals so I thought you might like to come along and watch.'

'I'd love to. What shall I wear?'

'Come as you are, apart from the feet. Gum boots would be best or old shoes.'

'How long do you think it will take?'

'It's difficult to say. If it's an easy one, we should be back here in an hour. If it's not so easy, it could be two or three hours. It won't be more than that, because if it's too tough, it'll need a caesarian and I shall have to come back to get the instruments.'

'Do you do many caesarians on cows?'

'It varies. We might go two or three months without having to do one and then perhaps have two in one week. One record is three in one weekend and all on the same farm. The farmer used a Sussex bull on a bunch of Friesian heifers. He fed them too well and by the time they were due to calve they were too fat and had oversized calves. They all had trouble calving, and we had to do caesars on five of the twelve. We'd better get a move on now. We don't want to keep the old girl waiting. She might go ahead and calve on her own then we shouldn't be able to charge the farmer.'

I hooted on the horn to announce our arrival. The cowman appeared at the door of the dairy.

'You'll want a bucket of hot water. Won't you?'

'Yes please Tom. I've got my own disinfectant, better than the stinking stuff you use around here.'

'There's nothing wrong with our disinfectant,' said Tom. 'It's good and strong.'

'I'll say it is. It'll burn a hole in the concrete. I'm not going to have it on my lily-white skin. How do you think the cow feels about it? Let's go and have a look at her. Which box is she in?'

We followed him through the dairy and across the yard behind, to a line of loose boxes. I looked over the half-door of the one with a light on. The cow, a big-boned Friesian was standing and had an anxious look about her. When she moved round the box, I could see just one foot of the calf.

'Tie her up with a head collar, over in that corner. Not too short, in case she decides to go down. I'll go and get my things on.'

The rubber of the calving apron was cold and clammy against my bare chest. I collected the disinfectant, soap and lubricating jelly and returned to the cow.

61

Anne and the cowman were leaning over the door, looking at her.

'How many calves has she had,' I asked looking at the rings on her horns. 'Two or three?'

'This will be her third. We had to help her a bit with the first one, but she didn't do badly for a heifer. She had the second on her own, cleansed and everything—no trouble.'

I asked the cowman to hold her tail on one side while I washed her off. He held on to the tail and leant against the cow's flank, partly to rest himself and also to stop the cow swinging about.

I washed my hands and arms, smeared them with lubricating jelly and took hold of the foot of the calf. I traced my hand up its leg and felt its knee.

'It's a front leg, so it's coming the right way round,' I said.

Sliding my hand further up the leg I felt the point of the shoulder and then the side of the neck. The head was bent right back, out of reach and was probably lying against its flank. By stretching my arm I could just feel an ear.

I would have to take off the apron as the sleeve got in the way. I needed those few extra inches to get hold of its head and turn it straight.

'Will you get me a sack and a bit of binder twine to protect my trousers,' I asked.

Re-lubricating my arm I started again and found the ear. By stretching forward with my cheek bone in intimate contact with the cow's rump, I found the other ear and eye. The dried dung on the hairs of her rump rasped quietly against my cheek. I slid my hand down the nose, found and gripped the lower jaw and gently eased the head round. She was a big cow and there was plenty of room in which to manoeuvre. Had she been smaller or if the cowman had left her too long, it would have been far more difficult. The uterus would have contracted down on to the calf and there would have been no room to turn the head.

I got the head straight with the nose just entering the pelvis. I then felt around for the other leg, which was folded back underneath the calf. I got hold of it to bring it up into line with the other leg, but it didn't feel right. Sliding my hand further along, I found a hock joint. This was a hind leg.

'You've got twins here,' I told the cowman.

'Are they alive?'

'The first one is, at the moment. It was sucking my thumb when I got hold of its jaw. I don't know about the other one. All I can feel is one of its hind legs. We'll get the one that's coming the right way round first and sort the other one out afterwards.'

I let go of the hind leg and moved my hand back to the neck of the first calf. I had to feel around for some time before I eventually found the missing leg. It was tucked back under its chest and behind the other elbow. I eased it gently across to its proper side. Moving my grip to its fetlock, I unfolded the leg and brought it up until it was lying alongside the other one, both small hooves protruding through the vulva.

'Would you like to lend a hand?' I asked Anne. 'You can pull on one leg while I pull on the other. Tom can stay on the tail. We don't want her lashing that around. It shouldn't be too difficult, as they're twins they'll be fairly small.'

Anne gingerly took hold of the indicated leg which was now protruding six inches.

'You'll need to keep up a steady tension until she strains, then pull harder. She should be able to calve on her own now it's straightened out, but it would take her longer. If we hurry things up, there will be a better chance of getting the other one out alive.'

Anne had one hand round the calf's foot and the other round its fetlock.

'I can't pull very hard. It's too slippery.'

'Hang on a minute and I'll get a couple of calving ropes.'

I collected them together with two wooden handles, which had once been part of a broomstick, from the car. Each rope had a loop at one end. I made a running noose, slipped it over the calf's foot and drew it tight above the fetlock. I turned the loose end round the wooden handle and handed it to Anne.

'That will make it easier for you.'

I repeated the performance with the other rope, stood

shoulder-to-shoulder with Anne and waited for the cow to strain. I noticed a small scab on the lobe of her ear, showing through the strands of auburn hair.

'Who's been biting your ear?'

'I had them pierced the other day, and that one went a bit septic. I ought to keep a small ring in it but it's too sore.'

'You ought to have gone to a good vet. He'd have made a much better job of it.'

The cow gave a heaving strain. It was accompanied by a moan which tailed off to a short grunt. The calf's legs came out a few more inches. I let go of my rope, rinsed and lubricated my arm and felt inside to check that the head was still in position.

'It shouldn't be long now. She's got enough room in there to drive a bus through. Once we get the head out the worst will be over. There might be a bit of trouble at the end, as it's a Friesian. They usually have bloody great hips.'

The cow strained four or five more times at short intervals. A pink tongue followed by a wet black nose appeared. I poked my finger up its nostrils to clear away the mucus.

'Go easy with the pulling now. We don't want to tear her. Let her do most of the work at this stage.'

The dome of the head appeared after an extra strong and prolonged heave. The long damp eyelashes flickered and its eyes opened. They didn't appear to focus on anything.

Anne was gazing, fascinated, mesmerised, at the calf's head.

'Come on. Snap out of it. We haven't finished yet.'

There was wonder in her eyes. She looked and sounded like a small schoolgirl.

'I didn't think its eyes would be open. Look. It's moving its tongue. Isn't it sweet.'

The shoulders and chest followed smoothly. The calf hung down limply, held by its hips.

'You'd better help pull now,' I told the cowman. 'You take this rope while I support its chest. Now both of you pull hard.'

While they were pulling, I rotated the calf slightly to get its hips level. The cow gave a final heave and a short strident bellow of pain as the hips came through her pelvis. The calf slumped out heavily, partly supported by my arms. It lay in the straw while I removed the ropes from its legs.

'Take it round to the front of the cow and let her lick it clean. It'll give her something to do while I'm sorting out the other one.'

The cowman took hold of the calf's front legs and pulled it through the straw towards the cow's head. Before leaving it, he lifted up one hind leg and announced that it was a heifer.

'Let's hope the other one is too or she won't be much use to you,' I commented.

'Why is that?' asked Anne.

'If you have twins, and one of them is a heifer and the other a bull calf the heifer is usually a "freemartin". That is, she doesn't have a normal uterus and so is no use for breeding.'

'If the next one is a bull calf, what will you do with them?'

'They'll go for veal.'

Anne shuddered and looked at the calf. It was now lying contentedly in front of its mother being cleaned with long rasping licks of her tongue.

'I shall never eat veal again.'

'Are you going to stop drinking milk and eating butter? A lot of calves are killed so that milk and butter can be sold for human consumption. Let's make a start with number two. He'll be getting lonely in there on his own.'

The second one was easier. Both hind legs were within easy reach. I straightened them and one by one brought them out. Anne, now anxious to help, took hold of one and started to pull. I pulled on the other.

'We shouldn't need ropes this time. The second one's usually easier and as it's coming backwards, there'll be the hocks to hold on to. You can keep a firmer grip on them than you can on the front legs.'

A short, wet, black tail appeared, threshed feebly and then went limp. A few more heaves and pulls and the hip followed.

'Now we have to pull hard and get it out as quickly as we can. Once the umbilical cord is trapped by the cow's pelvis, the calf will lose its oxygen supply. It will start trying to breathe on its own and as its head is still inside the cow, it will inhale a lot of fluid and may drown.'

In a matter of a few seconds, with all three of us pulling, the second calf was born. I picked up a handful of dry straw and rubbed its chest vigorously to induce it to start breathing. After a few preliminary flutters, the movement of its flanks settled down to a steady rhythm.

'Is it another heifer?' Anne asked hopefully.

'Have a look for yourself.'

'I'm not sure what to look for.'

I lifted up one of its hind legs and let it drop again.

'You're lucky. It is.'

The cowman brought me a fresh bucket of water to wash in.

'How did you enjoy your first calving case?' I asked Anne.

'I thought it was wonderful, fascinating. You are lucky being able to do this sort of work.'

'It's not very fascinating about five in the morning, when it's cold, dark and raining and the cow happens to be in the middle of a field.'

Before driving off, I wound down the window and spoke to the cowman.

'She should be all right tonight, Tom. Watch her tomorrow and especially tomorrow night. She may decide to go down with milk fever. It's her third calf, you know. If she hasn't cleansed in a couple of days, ring us up.'

'What's milk fever?' asked Anne, as we drove off.

'The correct name is Hypocalcaemia. It isn't a fever, in that the cow doesn't run a temperature. Basically, it's a sudden drop in the calcium level in the blood stream. The cow will have been dry for several weeks before calving; not giving any milk at all. Suddenly she starts churning out five or six gallons a day. Milk contains a lot of calcium. It's a considerable strain on her system to have to supply all this calcium at short notice. Sometimes the strain is too great and she can't maintain the proper level in her blood. When this happens, she begins to lose control of her legs. She staggers around as though she was drunk, then goes into a coma and, if not treated, dies.'

'How do you treat her?'

'We give an injection of calcium. Subcutaneously, which means under the skin. If she's flat out and we want it to act quickly, we give it directly into a vein; intravenously. That way, it gets right into the blood-stream and rapidly brings up the calcium level to normal. It can be quite spectacular. The cow can be lying flat out in a coma and in less than an hour she can be standing up, looking normal.'

'You told that man at the farm to ring you if she hadn't cleansed. What did you mean by that?'

'Cleansing means getting rid of the afterbirth or foetal membranes. Each calf has its own set, so she'll have two lots to get rid of. Oddly enough, if a cow has twins, she's much more likely to hold on to the afterbirths. If they're left in her for more than two days they can go rotten and cause a lot of trouble. I've known cows which have hung on to their cleansing for over a week, because the farmer hasn't bothered to call us. It smells a bit ripe by then. The cow gets pretty sick and sometimes dies. A mare won't tolerate her afterbirth nearly so well. If she hasn't cleansed in twelve hours, she's in real trouble.'

'Why doesn't the farmer call you in earlier? It seems silly to risk his cow's life.'

'He keeps hoping that she'll get rid of it on her own. Then he won't have to pay us to remove it. When his cow gets really sick, he gets worried. Sometimes he's too late.'

'It's not always pleasant being a vet, is it? To do your work, you must love animals.'

'Do you say the same to your doctor? Do you say you must love humans, being a doctor?'

'That's not the same.'

'I think it is. I think we're both motivated by the same thing. It's not love, it's interest, a professional, clinical interest. I neither like nor dislike the majority of my patients. For some, I have considerable affection, having got to know them in the course of treating them. Then there are some with an unpleasant temperament, almost human in fact. I actively dislike these, but when they're sick or injured, I'm interested in all of them.'

'Anyway, I think you're much cleverer than a doctor. Animals can't tell you where the pain is. You have to find out for yourself.'

'Animals don't want time off to go to a football match and pretend they've got a bad back. Animals don't suffer from "Plumbi oscillans" or lead-swinging. The poor bloody doctor has to sort out the wheat from the chaff.'

I stopped the car outside her house.

'Would you like to come in for a drink?'

'Thank you, but I'd better press on. I'm on duty and some other calls may have come in.'

'Thank you for taking me. It's been wonderful.'

'I trust we shall meet again round the rear end of some cow.'

CHAPTER EIGHT

MILK FEVER

IT was five in the morning when the phone rang. It was warm in bed, dark and cold outside. I lifted the receiver and managed a sleepy 'yes'.

It was Tom, the cowman from Lower Hone Farm. He sounded agitated and out of breath.

'Can you come as quick as you can. It's Petunia, the one you calved the other day. She's flat out and already started to blow up. I don't like the look of her at all.'

When you get a cow that's blown, every minute counts. I leapt out of bed, pulled on trousers, shirt and an old sweater and was on my way in five minutes. The roads were deserted and I ignored the speed limit. Screeching to a halt on the concrete apron in front of the dairy, I hurriedly changed into my boots and brown overall. I collected the injection apparatus and two bottles of calcium solution from the boot of the car and ran with them through the dairy and into the yard behind. I had assumed that the cow was in one of the calving boxes. The yard was empty and there was no sign of the cowman. I stood, irresolutely, in the early morning silence. A horrible feeling dawned on me that, being only half awake when I had answered the phone, I had mistaken the cowman's voice. It could have been some other cowman from some other farm. Whoever it was had been in a hurry and out of breath. I made a mental note that in future, however great the urgency, I would ask for the name of the farm and the farmer.

I walked back through the dairy, wondering what to do next. As I got to the car, I heard a distant shout. In the early dawn light, I recognised Tom, the cowman, waving his arms and running towards me across a field. I drove over the rutted grass to meet him.

'She's in the next field,' said Tom, still breathless. 'The gate's open. It's a bit rough in the gateway but you'll make it if you go steady. She's lying at the far side. After I phoned you, I went back to her to try and prop her up, but she's a big cow; too heavy for me to move on my own and too far gone, to help herself. She won't last much longer.'

'I told you to keep an eye on her. It's her third calf you know and she's a heavy milker—one of your best.'

'I kept her in the first two nights, so that she was handy and I could watch her. She seemed to be all right, so I turned her out with the rest of the herd after milking last night. I walked over and had a look at her before I went to bed. She was lying down so I hucked her up and made her walk round a bit. She looked fine, no sign of the staggers. Now this morning, when I go to get them in, there she is, flat out.'

I stopped the car a few feet from the recumbent cow. She was badly blown; her abdomen ballooned out tight as a drum. Lying on her side, she was unable to regurgitate or belch up the gas which was being continually formed in her rumen as part of her normal digestive process. Her tongue was protruding from her mouth but had not yet turned blue. It was however, only a question of minutes before the accumulating gas would distend the rumen to such an extent that the pressure of it on her diaphragm would make it impossible for her to breathe.

I hurriedly connected the injection apparatus to one of the bottles of calcium and took a large-bore intravenous needle from the steriliser.

'Have you got a length of binder twine or a bit of cord on you?' I asked. I normally carried a bit in the car, but had left it at some other farm.

He fumbled rapidly from pocket to pocket without success. I needed the cord to put round the cow's neck; drawn tight, it acted as a tourniquet and caused the jugular vein to fill up with blood. The distended vein was more easily recognised through the skin. It was also easier to get the needle properly into its lumen.

Time for the cow was running out. It would have taken too

long to go back to collect some from the dairy.

'Stick your clenched fist in there,' I told him, pointing at the jugular groove at the base of her neck. Slowly the vein started to fill out, as the return flow of blood was dammed up by the pressure of his fist. I tested it with my finger-tips and stuck the needle through the tough hide. No blood flowed. I withdrew it and tried again. I hit the vein and there was a steady flow of dark red blood, too dark for my liking. I up-ended the bottle of calcium and let the solution flow down the tubing to clear it of air bubbles before connecting it on to the needle. Then holding the bottle right up high, it got the maximum gravity flow. I waited, but there would be a time lag before the solution flowing into her vein took effect.

When the bottle was empty, I disconnected the rubber tubing and withdrew the needle from the vein. Having been given intravenously, the response was rapid. She showed signs of returning consciousness. The tetanic spasms in her legs relaxed and we were able to fold them under her body. Grasping her nostrils with two fingers and a thumb and her horn with my other hand, I pulled her head up off the ground towards me, while the cowman pushed against her withers. We propped her up on her brisket, but she was not conscious enough to maintain this position without support. We held her for a few moments. There was a deep, satisfying rumble of eructated gas which must have made her feel more comfortable and relieved us considerably. Several belches later, we let her go and her head slumped back on to the grass. I connected another bottle of calcium on to the infusion apparatus, stuck the same needle through the skin behind her elbow and let the fluid flow slowly into her. It was slower because it had to flow against the pressure of the tissues under the skin. There was now no degree of urgency and we were able to relax. I handed the bottle to the cowman and lit two cigarettes. I gave one to him. He was standing up, one arm held on high with the bottle like the Statue of Liberty. I sat down on the cow's backside and watched the level of the fluid slowly dropping in the bottle. When it was empty, I disconnected the tubing, pulled the needle out and pummelled the area with my fist to disperse the

71

fluid. Having packed the empty bottles and the injection apparatus away in the car, I returned to the cow and slapped her smartly on the rump with the flat of my hand. She responded by tossing her head up and scrabbling with her front feet until she had rolled herself on to her brisket. She produced another long and satisfying belch. The cowman went up to her, stroked her face and spoke to her by name. She was now safe to be left on her own. Within an hour or two, she would be up on her feet and walking around. It was only occasionally that the normal pattern of recovery failed to take place and additional injections were needed.

We drove back across the field to the dairy. I washed my hands and scrubbed and hosed down my boots before changing. I was just about to drive off, when the cowman came out of the dairy.

'While you're here, I wonder if you could have a look at a heifer that calved yesterday. I can't get any milk out of one of her quarters. She's all right on the other three and the teat feels all right on the blind one, but nothing comes out.'

I would have been more willing to see the heifer, and in a better frame of mind, if he'd told me about it before I'd changed, ready to drive off. I got out of the car, commenting peevishly that he'd have to wait while I changed into my boots again. He got the message. 'I've been so worried about Petunia that I'd forgotten about the heifer.'

She was in one of the loose-boxes in the yard behind the dairy. I left him to draw me off a fresh bucket of water, and set off to have a look at her on my own. The upper half-door of the end loose-box was open. I walked over to it and looked inside. There was a calf, lying contentedly in one of the far corners. Its mother, the newly calved heifer, had heard my approach. She turned and looked at me and gave a slight shake of her head as I watched her over the door. It should have been enough to warn me that she was 'calf proud' and therefore dangerous; potentially more dangerous than a bull, as she was lighter on her feet, less ponderous than a bull, hence she could move and turn more quickly. Being less alert than normal and impatient to get away, I failed to appreciate the warning signal. Without waiting for the cowman, I opened the door and walked right in. Pulling the door shut behind me, I walked across to her. She gave a low menacing moan, sounding like the growl of a large dog, and swung herself round. I then realised that I'd been more than careless to go into the box with her, being a stranger and without the support of the cowman, whom she would have recognised and been more likely to trust. I had also stupidly shut the door behind me. It was unnecessary to shut it, as she would never have left her calf.

She lowered her head and charged. I sidestepped in the thick straw but was not quick enough. One of her sharp, curved horns caught my trousers and tore into the pocket. There was a hot sharp stabbing pain in my thigh and I was flung against the wall. She held me pinned against the wall for a brief moment before tossing her head up. Still caught up with my trousers impaled on her horn, I was lifted bodily upwards with my back flat and hard against the flinty wall. She held me there, dangling lopsidedly about two feet clear of the floor. She then dropped me down and with an angry bellow, tossed her head up again. Once more my back rasped up the wall and I was held, suspended on high. A bucket dropped in the yard outside and there was the sound of running feet. The cowman burst into the box. He was carrying a stick and he clouted the heifer across the base of her unengaged horn. I felt the wind of it as it whistled past my ear. The heifer lowered her head and backed away. I collapsed in a heap on the soiled straw. He clouted her again and harder, across the nose. She backed further away towards the corner where her calf, watching the events with apparent disinterest, lay undisturbed. I took this opportunity to crawl out of the box. When I was clear of the doorway, the cowman backed out after me with his stick held ready until he'd shut and bolted the door. I stood up, thanked him and surveyed the damage. My trousers were torn right round to the seat, but they'd held my weight the second time she'd tossed me. If they'd let me down, I would probably have got a horn through my guts. A thin trickle of warm blood ran down my thigh. The wound was not deep and all things considered, I'd got off pretty lightly.

The cowman supported me by one elbow and asked if I was all right.

'I should have warned you about her, but I didn't think that you'd go into the box until I arrived with the water. She's a bit hot. She nearly got me yesterday; that's why I was carrying this stick. Luckily, I heard her bellow, so I guessed something was up.'

With real affection, I patted him on the shoulder.

'You were right about something being up. It was me, half-way up the bloody wall. It was my own fault. I should have had more sense than to walk into a box with a newly calved heifer without watching and waiting to see how she would behave. I saw her shake her head at me and didn't take the warning. I need my brains tested.'

'We'll leave her for a bit to settle down,' said the cowman. 'Come into the dairy and wash up.'

We decided to leave the heifer until the afternoon, to give all three of us a chance to settle down. I drove home, changed my trousers and turned up late for morning surgery.

The limp, possibly slightly exaggerated, was noticed and commented upon by Mike, the junior partner.

'What's happened to you? Shot by a jealous husband or did you merely fall out of somebody's bed?'

I described the morning's events and received no sympathy. My suggestion that he might like to visit and examine the heifer himself fell on stony ground. He felt that it would be unethical to take over another veterinary surgeon's case.

I returned to the farm after lunch. With a slight sense of trepidation I enquired after the heifer. The cowman enquired after my leg. The heifer had settled down and he'd moved her into another box, away from her calf, so that her maternal instinct would be less aggressive. She was tied up short with a good and strong rope halter. He'd been in to see her several times, talked to her and run his hand over her udder. She had shown no resentment, but he still couldn't get any milk out of one of her quarters.

I enquired after Petunia. She had got up about an hour after we had left her and walked down to the dairy on her own. I advised him not to strip her right out for the next few days, in case she went down with milk fever again.

The heifer was standing quietly, feeding from the hay rack in front of her. I spoke to her and ran my hand along her back and down her flank; a move which appeared to be less ticklish and caused less resentment than the more direct approach up her thigh. Handling her udder gently, I tried each teat in turn. The off-side front one felt normal but produced no milk.

The cowman fitted a pair of 'Bulldogs' into her nose. These were tied with several thicknesses of binder twine on to the upper rail of the hay rack in front of her. As she was pulled up close to the rail, I noticed that she still had some blood, my blood, dried and flaky, on the tip of one horn. I cleaned off the end of her teat with disinfectant and took a thin metal canula from the steriliser. Before inserting it up the streak canal of the blocked teat. I got the cowman to push her tail up and forward over her back to diminish the effect of any kick she might feel inclined to give.

On insertion, the canula met with no opposition and caused no resentment on the heifer's part, until it reached the top of the teat, where it joined the udder. A short, sharp jab upwards, popped it through a membrane. A thin stream of thick yellow fluid ran out. The cowman would have called it 'beastings'; its proper name was 'colostrum'. It was not normal milk and could not be sold as such. It was the first few days' secretion from the udder of a newly-calved cow or heifer. It was heavily laced with antibodies which gave the newly born and vulnerable calf its early protection against disease. I left the canula in position for several minutes to relieve the pressure in the quarter. While the flow continued, I explained to the cowman that there was a membrane across the top of the teat which was interfering with the flow of milk. The small hole made by the canula would close up when it was withdrawn. It would be necessary to tear a much larger hole in the membrane to get a reasonable flow of milk down into the teat.

In the steriliser was an instrument that looked like a blunt ended cork-screw. The canula was removed from the teat and, once more, the heifer's tail was pushed up and over her back. She was a young heifer and not vicious, except in her instinct to defend her calf. So, in spite of the fact that the next operation was going to be painful for her, we decided not to submit her to the additional discomfort of having her legs tied. The spiral was twisted up her teat until it was clear of the narrow milk canal. It moved freely up the lumen of the teat until it reached the obstructing membrane at the top. I stabbed the point of the instrument through the membrane, which she resented slightly, and screwed the corkscrew part through. Warning the cowman to hold tight, I stood back and gave the instrument a short, sharp downward wrench. It ripped the membrane free. The heifer jumped, both hind feet leaving the ground. Having her tail pushed up made it difficult for her to kick and the speed of the operation took her by surprise. She swung away from me and the teat spiral was left swinging free. We let her alone for a few minutes to settle down before screwing the spiral out through the canal. I told the cowman to try and milk her. She had forgotten the brief interlude of pain and appeared to bear him no ill-will.

The first few pulls were heavily blood-stained and looked more like raspberry juice than milk, but there was no longer any obstruction in the flow. Once the blood had cleared the farmer would have a normal four-quarter heifer.

CHAPTER NINE

URGENT CASES

ONE evening after surgery, the door-bell rang. Not an unusual occurrence, as clients frequently ignored the official surgery times.

Anne was standing on the door-step clutching a brown paper bag.

'Am I too late?'

'It depends what you want. Come in.'

'They told me at the stables that my mare, Cherry, might have redworms. They said if I took a sample of her droppings, they could be checked.' She held up the paper bag. 'Can you do it?'

I looked at my watch. 'I guess so. We normally go through a batch of them after morning surgery. Come into the lab.'

I weighed out a precise amount of the droppings and put it into a small screw-top jar which already contained about a dozen glass beads. I added a quantity of a solution of sugar and water, screwed the top on and gave it a vigorous shaking. The glass beads broke up the semi-solid mass until it was more or less homogeneous liquid. I strained it into a beaker. Using a special glass slide with a central chamber marked off with squares etched in the glass, I examined a sample of the liquid under a microscope. Six, thin-walled oval eggs were visible within the marked off area.

'She's got a heavy enough infestation to warrant treating her. In this sample there are 600 eggs per gram. Over two hundred they ought to be treated.'

'How can you tell that?' she asked.

'The dilution is worked out so that each egg on the slide represents 100 in each gram of droppings. They float up in the sugar solution so that they're all visible under the cover-slip of the slide.'

'Can I have a look?' she asked.

I got off the stool and let her peer down the microscope.

'I can't see anything. What am I supposed to be looking for?'

'Worm eggs. They're oval and transparent. You should be able to make out the thin outline of the casing also the small larval worm curled up inside. Let me adjust it for you.'

She moved her head to one side. I bent down close to her and moved the slide so that two worm eggs were in the field of vision.

'Now have a look. Turn the knob on the side. It will adjust the focus to suit your eyes. There's one egg in the very middle of the field and another down about four o'clock.'

'Yes. I can see them now. Can those tiny little things do so much harm?'

'When they've hatched out and grown up, several thousand of them can do a lot of damage. They bury their heads in the wall of the intestine and it becomes inflamed which interferes with digestion. They also sometimes burrow right through it into the blood vessels. They get thickened walls which interferes with the blood supply to the intestines and the horse becomes a poor do-er, and subject to attacks of colic.'

'Do they grow very big?'

I told her that there were three species of strongyle in the horse. 'When adult they vary in length from half to one and a half inches. Ascarid worms are much bigger. About ten inches long and greyish white in colour. They are much more serious in foals. If you plan to breed from your mare, I suggest that you worm her for ascarids, as the larval form can penetrate the placental barrier and infest the foal before it's born.'

The phone rang. I left her sitting in the lab while I answered it. It was a police call. Urgent. A horse involved in an accident with a car. I called out to Anne.

'Panic stations. There's a horse been hit by a car out on the road to Ash Farm. Do you want to come?'

I unlocked a drawer in the office desk and took out a .38 revolver. I checked that it was unloaded and put three bullets in my jacket pocket. As I walked out of the room Anne was standing in the doorway.

'What are you going to do with that?' she asked apprehensively.

'Use it on the horse. Maybe.'

She shuddered. 'How horrible.'

'Road accidents often are horrible. Do you still want to come along?'

'Yes. I'll come, but I think I'll stay in the car.'

I pulled on to the grass verge, just short of the accumulated cars. There was a tense atmosphere and a sense of drama in the scene, accentuated by the monotonous flashing electric blue light of a police car. Long black skid marks pointed accusingly at a saloon car which lay at their end. A policeman directed the inquisitive traffic past the obstruction.

On the other side of the car, I could see a horse standing with a man at its head. I walked towards it and looked briefly at the front of the saloon as I passed it. The windscreen and one head lamp were shattered. The wing and radiator grill were pushed well back on to the engine.

A policeman came over and spoke to me.

'Are you the vet, sir?'

'Yes,' I answered.

'It looks pretty nasty to me, sir.'

I nodded and we walked towards the horse.

It looked pretty nasty to me too. There was a gaping pink wound, nine inches long, just below the stifle joint. Blood was oozing from it gently and caking on the hairs down the leg. This wound was only skin deep, and would have been a simple matter to suture. There would be little point in attending to it. Further down and below the hock the leg was broken. A sharp white sliver of bone stuck out through the skin. The lower part of the leg, connected only by the extensor tendon and a strip of twisted skin, looked sickeningly incongruous. The foot was facing the wrong way and was swinging like a slow pendulum.

I went up to its head and stroked it on the muzzle. It had a resigned, world-weary expression in its eyes, as in a human who had been weeping and was about to weep again.

I asked the man holding on to its head-collar who the owner was. He didn't know for sure. He thought it might belong to Mrs Brown who rented a field down the road as summer grazing for her two hunters.

'There's no question of repairing that leg,' I said to the policeman. 'The sooner we put the poor sod out of his misery, the better. I'll go and get the gun. I'll get on to the knacker to collect the body as soon as I get back to the surgery.'

I turned to walk away and bumped into Anne. She'd walked quietly up to the scene and was standing right behind me. She looked pale and shocked. I took her by the arm and led her back to the car.

'I think it will be better if you stay in the car.'

'Are you going to shoot him?'

'There's nothing else I can do. That leg would never mend.'

I took the gun and walked back to the horse. The policeman moved the onlookers away from the horse and out of the line of fire. I broke the gun, put one round up the spout and snapped it shut. Standing directly in front of the horse's head, I visualised two lines drawn from the base of each ear to the opposite eye. I held the muzzle of the gun an inch above the point where the two lines would have crossed. I kept it clear of the skin and hair, pointed it slightly upwards and gently squeezed the trigger.

On the drive back Anne remained silent. When we got to the surgery, I called through to Mike who was phone-sitting for me. I told him about the horse and asked if anything else had happened.

'About ten minutes ago a woman brought in a choking cat. I told her we'd deal with it and phone her back. It's all yours.'

The cat was in a fibre-glass box in the examination room. It was commenting loudly on its incarceration, as Siamese cats do.

I put on a white coat, washed my hands and lifted it out of the box. It crouched on the table and looked anxiously at the strange surroundings. It was on unfamiliar territory, and was not as confident and aggressive as it would have been if it was playing at home. I stroked its head and talked to it with a cat accent. It was too concerned with its own discomfort to pay much attention. It was dribbling profusely; long, glutinous strands hung from the corner of its mouth and its chin was wet and soggy. It arched its back and retched, but it produced only a nauseating croak and more saliva.

'It could be a bad tooth, a bone stuck in its throat or an attack of cat flu. Siamese cats seem particularly susceptible to cat flu and the symptoms can appear very suddenly. We'll have a look.'

I spoke to it again and stroked its head to allay some of its fear. I then opened its mouth. The cat brought up a paw with the claws half unsheathed. Anne moved forward.

'Shall I hold him to stop him scratching you?'

'No. Leave him alone. No cat likes being restrained. He's not really trying to claw me, just holding hands. It'll make him happier to let him do it. There's something at the back of his throat. It looks like a bit of cotton and bits of cotton often have needles attached to them. We shall have to give him pentothal to examine him properly. I'll phone up his owners to get their permission. You hold on to the kitty.'

I came back from the phone.

'They said go ahead and do what you think best. Can you lend me a hand to give him the anaesthetic? I'll show you how to hold him.'

I filled a small syringe with pentothal.

'The injection has to be given into a vein. Normally in cats and dogs we use the one that runs up the front of the forearm. If you miss the vein and the injection goes outside it, apart from not anaesthetising the cat, you get the father and mother of all abscesses.'

With a pair of curved scissors, I clipped short the hair up the front of its leg. I cleaned the skin with a cotton-wool swab soaked in antiseptic.

'I want you to hold up this leg. Grip it fairly tightly below the elbow to bring up the vein. Your hand will act as a tourniquet and the vein will fill up with blood. That will make it easier to see and easier to get the needle into it. When I say "let go", release the pressure of your grip.'

I held the syringe vertically up to the light and gently

pushed up the plunger to eliminate any bubbles. I held the cat's paw in my left hand, felt the distended vein and pushed the needle through the skin. The cat jerked its leg back and the needle came out.

'You'll have to hold him tighter. Cradle his head in your other hand, in case he decides to bite the syringe or me.'

I started again and got into the vein. I injected a little of the anaesthetic rapidly, and within seconds I felt the cat begin to relax. I paused and then injected some more. The cat became lightly unconscious, lying flat on the table. With my free hand, I eased his tongue out of his mouth, to facilitate his breathing. I watched his respirations for a few moments and gave him a bit more anaesthetic. I withdrew the needle and spoke to Anne.

'Pass me that small torch over there. We'll see what we can see.'

Anne stood watching the cat.

'He looks dead to me.'

I opened the cat's mouth and pulled the tongue out.

'Shine the light down its throat.'

I pulled the tongue out even further.

'That looks interesting. Silly kitty, playing with a needle and cotton.'

Anne peered over my shoulder.

'What is it?'

'He's got a needle embedded in the base of his tongue. There's only the eye showing.'

She looked incredulous.

'How did it get there?'

'It's not all that uncommon. They start playing with the cotton. They lick it and keep on swallowing it until they get to the needle at the end. They start to swallow that too. Sometimes they do. Other times, when the eye of the needle touches the sensitive back of the throat, they cough or retch and the needle shoots forward and sticks in the back of the tongue. Which is what happened in this case.'

I let go of the tongue and took a pair of Spencer-Wells artery forceps from a wall cabinet. Anne opened its mouth and pulled the tongue forward again. I clamped the forceps on to the eye of the needle and pushed it backwards down its throat. When the point of the needle came clear, I pulled it up again with about ten inches of wet cotton.

'That should make him feel a bit more comfortable.' I held on to the end of the cotton and swung the needle to and fro.

'We'll keep this to show the owner.'

The cat was beginning to come round from the anaesthetic. He twitched his whiskers and made tentative efforts to lick his nose.

'We'll let him stay here tonight. I'll phone the owners to tell them all is well. There are some cages in the next room. While I'm phoning, will you put a clean sheet of paper in one of them? Take the kitty through and lay him flat on his side, as he is now.'

When I came back from the phone, Anne was still in the kennel room, watching the cat through the wire mesh of the cage door.

'He's trying to lift his head. He looks very bleary-eyed.'

'I look like that every morning.'

'Will he be all right? Left in here on his own tonight?'

'He'll be better off in here. Better than going home when he's still dopey. When they're coming round from an anaesthetic, they start trying to walk too soon. They find they're all staggery, try and run and then get in a panic. He may still be a bit wobbly on his pins tomorrow, but not enough to do any harm.'

The phone rang.

It was a small tenant-farmer. He was worried that one of his cows wasn't getting on with the calving as she ought to. He only milked twelve cows and could ill afford to lose one. A live calf was also important, especially if it was heifer.

Anne was still watching the cat.

'We're having a busy night. That was a calving case. Do you want to come and watch?'

She looked doubtful.

'I'd love to, but it's getting pretty late. I think I'd better miss this one.'

CHAPTER TEN

A HORSE WITH COLIC

IT was nearly midnight when I turned the car off the road. I had to untie a ragged piece of binder twine which served a double purpose; keeping the farmyard gate shut and stopping it from falling down. A similar piece of twine had taken over the duty of the rusted and useless hinges at the other end. I let the car roll into the enclosed yard and tooted the horn.

Some moments later a dim light appeared in a far corner. It strengthened and materialised into a storm lantern, which swung erratically towards me. The farmer apologised for having called me out so late.

'We noticed that she was springing this afternoon, but she isn't due until tomorrow and we thought that she'd go through the night. I went out to have a look at her before I turned in, and saw that she'd got her water-bag showing. I watched her for another hour and as she didn't seem to be getting on with it, I thought I'd better call you.'

In the short time that I'd been in the practice, I had been out to this farm several times. The farmer had accepted me on my first visit and I liked him for it. In spite of the late hour, I was prepared to be pleasant. I liked calving cases anyway; the sense of satisfaction and achievement in producing a live calf more than compensated for the discomfort and late working. The fact that the cow's gait and posture had altered due to the pelvic ligaments slackening off was enough to alert the farmer that she was approaching or 'springing' to calve. It was not in itself any cause for immediate concern, as some cows would go on another two or three days before they actually started calving. It was the amnion or foetal membranes containing the amniotic fluid, which the farmer called the water-bag, bulging out through the lips of the cow's vulva which induced him to phone.

A bucket of hot water, a piece of soap and a towel were produced I followed the farmer and his lantern across the muddy yard to a loose-box on the other side. By heaving his weight against the lower half of the door, he was able to shift the rusty bolt which held it shut against a foot-high tide of well-rotted manure. I followed him up into the box and waited while he tied the cow up to a hay rack in one corner. He held the cow's tail to one side while I lubricated my arm. The water bladder had already broken and in the dim light of the lantern, I saw a relatively normal though rather wet looking cow's crotch. I washed it and inserted my left hand. Two small hooves lay comfortably and only just inside the pelvis. Above and a few inches behind them was a wet nose and sharp incisor teeth. The cow strained and the feet and nose moved easily towards me. This was an uncomplicated calving case. Had I been a quarter of an hour later, she would have calved on her own.

'How is it?' enquired the farmer anxiously.

'We'll manage it all right,' I assured him. As the cow strained again, I pushed hard against the calf's head. I continued the delaying tactics for several minutes.

'What's holding it up?' he asked, with increasing anxiety.

I lied competently, with the confidence of a professional man.

'The head's not coming right, but we'll soon get it organised.'

I let her strain a few more times and then stopped opposing her. With the next effort on the cow's part, the calf slid out easily, not even delayed by its hips. I broke its fall with my forearms, gave it a brisk rub with a handful of straw and pulled it round to the head of the cow to let her lick it.

After changing, I accepted the offer of a cup of tea and a wash in the farmhouse kitchen. The farmer's wife, in her broken-down carpet slippers and wrinkled grey stockings, fussed over me affectionately on hearing that both cow and calf were doing well.

Later that morning, at a little after seven o'clock, the phone rang. It was Anne. I lay back on the pillow with the receiver cradled against my ear.

'Did I wake you up? I'm off to the stables now and I wondered how you got on with the calving last night.'

'No trouble at all. I was back here and in bed by ten to one. She didn't need any help. In fact I had to push against her for about ten minutes to stop her calving too quickly.'

'What did you do that for?'

'To make it appear more difficult than it really was.'

'Why?'

'To impress the farmer and to make him think that he was getting good professional value for his money.'

'But that's not fair. In fact it sounds very dishonest to me,' said Anne sounding shocked and disillusioned.

'What do you suggest I should have done? Tell the farmer that she could calve on her own, that she didn't need any help and that he was a bloody fool to have called me out so late and for nothing?'

'You could have explained to him. Politely.'

'Look. This farmer is a nice type, but not very bright. However polite I'd been, he'd have been self-conscious about calling me out for nothing. So the next time he's got a cow having trouble calving, he's going to be frightened of making a mistake. He'll leave her for several hours and end up with a dead cow or calf or both, and that means a lot to a small farmer. As it is, he's got a live cow and calf. He won't be charged any more because I chose to delay the moment of its birth.'

She then asked me if she could pick up the worm medicine for her mare, which she had forgotten.

'I'll make it up for you when I get to the surgery.'

My last call of the day, before surgery, was to a little thatched cottage, occupied by a small, bright-eyed, grey-haired spinster.

She kept bees, chickens and a goat. The goat had not had a kid for over three years, yet continued to give about a pint of milk a day, which was enough for the owner. It needed its feet trimming. It had always been temperamental and as it grew older, it became more so. The owner used to take it up the lane on a collar and chain to graze from the hedgerows. It had got too much for her to control, was now confined to its pen and its feet, through lack of exercise, had become overgrown.

It did not welcome strangers and strongly resented having its feet handled. It reared up, bleated, fell down, struggled up and repeatedly jerked its foot out of my grasp as I tried to pare the overgrown horn. I was sweating profusely by the time all four feet were trimmed. She offered me a glass of home-made barley water and invited me to look at her chickens. There were nearly two dozen Light Sussex hens scratching around in a large run. They looked healthy and happy. Strutting importantly in the same run were two cockerels, one Light Sussex and one Rhode Island.

Before I left, she presented me with half a dozen large, brown eggs. She assured me that she had far too many for her own use. She was considering putting a card up in the local general store, advertising clutches of eggs from pure Light Sussex stock, for hatching.

I pointed out to her that there might be some confusion and cross-breeding as there was also the Rhode Island in the same run.

She assured me that there was no possibility of that occurring. She was always very careful and made sure that he was shut away in a separate pen at night. I didn't have the heart to enlighten her.

Towards the end of surgery, Anne called for the worm treatment for her mare. It was my night off duty and I invited her to have a drink.

The saloon bar of the Crown was crowded. I left her at a table and fought my way up to the bar. On my way back, clutching a glass in each hand, a large domineering lady, wearing sensible brogues, tweed skirt and small moustache, placed herself squarely in my path.

'I've been wanting to see you,' she announced in a loud voice. 'It's about my little "Po". He keeps scraping along the ground on his bottom. Do you think he's got worms? He's always licking his private parts too.'

The hubbub in the bar died suddenly. The occupants waited

for my learned pronouncement on 'Po's' personal complaints.

I put on a small, professional smile and suggested that she bring him to the surgery in the morning.

'He's outside in the car. Couldn't you look at him now?'

'It will be a little difficult to examine him in here. It will be more convenient in the surgery.'

'It's so difficult for me to get to your surgery. My mornings are always busy and I have committee meetings almost every evening. Could you visit him at my home?'

'I'll phone you tomorrow morning to fix a convenient time for me to visit you.'

I started to edge past her. She effectively countered this move.

'I'm afraid I shall be out all morning. Could you phone me at lunch time?'

'I'll phone you at lunch time.'

She let me go reluctantly. I squeezed my way to the table and slumped into a chair.

'You looked very cross,' said Anne. 'What did she want?'

'She wanted me to stick my finger up her dog's arse. I came here for a quiet drink, not to carry out consultations!'

'You wanted to be a vet. You must expect it.'

I was halfway through my pint when the landlord called me to the phone.

It was Mike from the surgery. He was just about to start a caesarian on a bitch and there was a call from Manor Stud. They had a horse with colic. He knew it was my evening off, but could I cope with it?

'What exactly is colic?' asked Anne, as we drove to the stud farm. 'I've heard them talk about it at the stables.'

'It's a general term for belly-ache. It can be anything from a mild flatulence to a twisted gut, which is usually fatal.'

'What's a twisted gut?'

'A section of the intestine gets itself kinked or twisted. The blood supply to that section also gets twisted and cut off. The tissues then die and go gangrenous.'

'How do you treat a twist?'

'A lead injection.'

'A what?'

'Shoot it.'

The owner and the head groom were waiting when we got to the stable yard.

'It's Proud Pasha. He was all right at six this evening, except that he didn't clear up his feed. He covered a mare this morning and seemed quite normal. Bill here came out and had a look at him at seven thirty, as he hadn't cleared his manger. He found him down and sweating. We rugged him up and walked him round but he still tries to go down and roll. We've only just put him back in his box.'

The groom took off the horse-blanket. I stood and looked at the horse for a few moments. He was sweating in patches, mainly on his flanks. After checking his pulse, I took off my hat, bent down and placed my ear against his sweat-stained flank. I listened for half a minute.

'Sounds like the Salvation Army Band in there and his pulse rate's up a little. I'll check his temperature.'

I eased up his tail and inserted the thermometer.

'Temperature's normal. Has he passed anything?'

'Not since we bedded him up at six. He's done a good bit of straining.'

'Get me a bucket of warm water, a bit of soap and a towel. I'll need a couple of straw bales too, in case he tries to kick my teeth in.'

I put on a rubber apron, filled my fingernails with soap and lathered it up my left arm. The stallion was backed up to the straw bales. Standing behind them, I lifted up his tail and gently inserted my hand. There was a thump which shook the bales as the horse protested. He then stood quietly. In easy stages I emptied his rectum, felt around and withdrew my arm. I examined it before I washed.

'I don't think you've got much to worry about. It's only a little wind that's churning up his guts. If he had anything more serious, like a twist or a bad stoppage, the linings of his rectum would have clung to my arm and there would have been small flecks of mucus on it. I'll give him an injection and stomach-tube him.'

Anne followed me out to the car. I handed her the stomach tube and pump and a bottle of brown medicine. She carried them to the loose-box while I filled a syringe with pethidine. Having given the injection, I got the groom to fetch me a clean bucket with a couple of quarts of cold water. I poured the brown medicine into it and mixed it with my hand. I then lubricated the end of the stomach tube with liquid paraffin.

'I shall need your help now, Anne. When I'm ready, will you fit the other end of this tube on to the pump, stick it in the bucket and start pumping.'

I rested one hand on the horse's nose and with the other pushed the tube up one of its nostrils. After about three inches, the horse shook its head and it came out. I started again and this time got in about six inches of the tube. The horse reared up on its hind legs and struck out with a fore-foot, just missing me. I turned and spoke to the groom.

'Will you come and lend a hand here? Stand the other side of him and hold on to his head.'

With some luck and the aid of the groom, I got the tube well in and pushed it up until it reached the back of its throat. I then moved the tube slowly up and down until the horse swallowed, then pushed it firmly for another twelve inches. I stood back half a pace and watched the side of the neck while continuing to push the tube slowly. The slight bulge moving down its gullet confirmed that it was in the right place and not in the windpipe. I pushed it rapidly on for another four feet and spoke to Anne.

'Now get cracking. Connect up and pump steadily. When the bucket's empty, take the tube off and hand it to me.'

She finished pumping and handed me the loose end. I put it in my mouth and blew down it to clear it.

'You've got to be careful that the horse doesn't blow first.'

Slowly, I pulled the tube out and let it fall on the floor. There were a few flecks of blood on it. Blood started to drip from the nostril. The horse snorted, blew down its nose and shook its head, splattering me with a fine red spray. The individual drops coalesced into a thin stream, staining the straw bedding. Anne looked at it with alarm.

'Will he be all right?'

'Absolutely. This often happens and I've never known one come to any harm. The mucous membrane lining the nose is very delicate. It's not unusual for the tube to damage it and, as you can see, it bleeds freely. In the old days they used to practise blood letting as a cure for colic, and practically everything else as well.'

I started to clean the stomach tube. I said to the groom. 'Rug him up again, walk him around for half an hour and then put him back in his box. Give him a couple of hours and if you're not happy about him then ring the surgery. There's not much to worry about. I think you'll find he'll be all right. Clear out his manger and leave him a bucket of water and a hay net to pick at.'

As soon as we were on the road Anne started firing questions.

'When you were examining him behind, why did you use your left hand?'

'I was advised to start off using my left hand when I was a student, learning to do pregnancy diagnosis on cows. In the spring, the flush of grass makes them pretty loose. It also contains a lot of chlorophyll. After examining several cows, you find that your hand and arm are stained green and it won't wash off. If you go to shake hands with someone and offer a green hand, it doesn't look very attractive. Hence the left hand.'

'It sounds awfully messy to me. Do you like doing it?'

'It's a living and it keeps one's hand warm in winter.'

'You really are revolting.'

'I'm a vet. Any more questions?'

'Yes. When you were pushing that tube up its nose, why were you watching the side of its neck so carefully?'

'To make absolutely certain that it was going down the right way. Down the oesophagus to the stomach and not the windpipe into its lungs. It's almost impossible to tell by feel. If you can see the bulge as it moves along the gullet, you can be certain that it's all right.'

'What would happen if it went down the wrong way?'

'You'd have pumped that half gallon of fluid into its lungs. That wouldn't have done it much good.'

'Have you ever made a mistake and done that?'

'No, I'm glad to say. I once saw a silly clot of an Army vet do it.'

'What happened?'

'The horse died. Rather unpleasantly by drowning.'

Anne shuddered and stopped talking.

CHAPTER ELEVEN

A DEAR LITTLE PEKE

'WE'VE got a nice one lined up for you this morning,' said Mike, when I arrived at the surgery.

'It came in about half an hour ago—Ash Farm. One of their heifers. By the sound of it, she's been trying to calve all night. They're lying out on the other side of the wood up there. They didn't notice this one until they went to feed them after milking. The cowman said he looked at them yesterday evening, but she could have started soon after that. If you think she needs a caesarian, phone us from the farm. We'll get the instruments ready.'

The cowman and the farmer's son were waiting for me outside the dairy.

'You'll have to leave your car here. We'll go up on the tractor. She's in Long Meadow, the other side of the woods. Is there anything you want to take with you?'

'We'd better take two buckets of hot water. By the time we get there, each one will be half full, if we're lucky. You can lend me a hand to move the stuff from my car.'

The calving box, instrument case and disinfectant were loaded on to the flat trailer hitched on the tractor. I climbed on and sat down on a straw bale. The cowman appeared from the dairy carrying the two buckets of water, climbed up and sat down beside me. The farmer's son mounted the tractor, coaxed it into life and drove off a little too fast for our comfort.

I offered the cowman a cigarette and lit it for him.

'How long do you think she's been at it?'

He drew deeply on his cigarette before replying.

'Er could 'av bin on all night. I can't understand it meself. I don't often go wrong. After milking yesterday evening, I 'ad me tea and walked up there with a gun. Thought I might see a rabbit in the woods. There's fourteen 'eifers up there. Counting from the time we put the bull in with them, they shouldn't be starting to calve for a couple o' weeks yet. We was going to bring 'em down 'andy to the dairy at the beginning of next week. There's two or three that's started to bag up but none on 'em was springing or even looking like it. Young 'Enery went up to feed 'em this morning. When 'e counted 'em there was one short. So 'e looks around and there she is, down at the far corner, calving. So 'e comes back and tells me. I went up on the tractor to 'ave a look at 'er meself. She's got the 'ead out. He looks dead to me.'

'No legs showing?'

'No, Just the 'ead. So I says to meself, this is a job for the vet.'

'What bull did you use on them?'

'An Angus, this time. He was a smart little chap. Light and quick worker. Not one on 'em turned. 'E caught 'em all first time. Last year we used an 'Ereford. We 'ad to get you people out to three or four on 'em. Dirty great big calves. I didn't think we'd 'ave any trouble this year.'

We sat smoking in silence as the trailer bumped over the rutted track. I looked back, down and across the field to the farmyard and the farmhouse lying beyond. It was a still, sunny morning. A finger of smoke rose vertically from one of the farmhouse chimneys. It merged into the background of tall elms with their attendant, circling rooks. It was a peaceful country scene, when viewed from afar. The harsh commercial reality of it was not immediately apparent, neither were the spiteful, bullying farmyard hens, the inconsiderate cattle nor the indolent and selfish sows.

The trailer stopped. The cowman jumped off, opened the gate into the field and shut it again after we'd passed through. He jumped back on as we moved across the field.

The heifers had congregated in a circle around the one who was trying to calve like a group of curious onlookers at the scene of a road accident. They retreated a little as the tractor approached and directed their soft-eyed, inquisitive stares from further back. They watched, not with compassion, but

94

with a detached, almost clinical interest.

Having clothed myself in a protective overall, I sank on my knees behind the heifer. The calf was very dead. Its head, which was all that was visible, was grossly distended. It had been dead for several hours. The heifer gave a half-hearted strain and moaned quietly. She had long since exhausted herself in her futile efforts to rid herself of the calf. She was near to collapse from exhaustion and shock.

I spoke to the farmer's son.

'You'd better go back to my car. If we're going to save her, she'll need some intravenous glucose saline. Look in the boot, you'll find a large two-litre bottle. And there's a metal steriliser with the injection apparatus in it. We'll also need a bit of cord or binder twine to bring up the vein in her neck. Be as quick as you can. While you're on your way, I'll start to remove the head. It's much too swollen to push back and we've got to get it out of the way to get the legs up, before we start pulling.'

He unhitched the trailer from the tractor and drove off at speed, leaving the gate open as he left the field. The rest of the heifers were too interested in the activity around the calving heifer to bother about escaping. We heard the high whine of the tractor as it went through the woods in top gear.

'You mark my words,' said the cowman. 'That young lad'll kill 'iself before 'e's much older.'

I grunted non-committally. I was already absorbed, threading the wire saw of the embrytome down one of the protecting tubes. I then had to thread it back down the other side tube, leaving a loop hanging at the end. I clamped two metal handles on to the loose ends of the wire and passed the whole apparatus over to the cowman to hold ready.

Going down on to my knees once more, I fitted the noose of the wire saw over the calf's head and eased back the lips of the cow's vulva to get it as far up the neck as possible.

'Start sawing now,' I told the cowman. 'Short pulls to begin with, until we get through the hair and skin. It'll clog up and drag a bit of the hair at first.'

I pushed the twin protecting tubes of the embrytome tight

95

up under the calf's chin, bracing it with both hands. The cow-man straddled his feet and pulled alternatively on each handle.

'You're right about it clogging up. I can hardly move it.'

'Keep on with the good work. You're almost through the skin now. When you feel it getting freer, increase your pull to about a foot each time. You'll go through the muscle and bone like a knife through butter.'

After half a dozen long, sweeping pulls, the wire saw rasped against the metal tubes and the calf's head rolled on to the grass. I let the embrytome drop, pushed the severed head out of the way and slid my hand up beside the stump of the calf's neck.

'She's pretty dry in here, but I think we'll manage now.'

Placing my other hand on the stump end of the neck, I tried to push the calf back to make enough room to get my arm in and locate the front legs. Every time I pushed, the heifer gave a half-hearted strain. It was a pathetic effort but was enough to defeat my object. I stood up and rinsed my hands and arm.

'We'll have to give her a spinal anaesthetic to stop her straining.'

I clipped the hair off an area of skin over the base of the tail, and cleaned it with an antiseptic swab. I then picked out a tough hypodermic needle, two and a half inches long, and filled a syringe with local anaesthetic. Placing a forefinger on the cleaned area, I moved the tail gently up and down like a pump handle to locate the gap between two of the bones of the tail. The needle went through the skin almost up to its hilt without difficulty. I connected the syringe on to it and pressed down the plunger. There was little or no resistance to the flow, which confirmed that the needle was correctly placed.

'It'll take a few minutes to act, so we'll have a cigarette while we're waiting.'

The tractor came bounding across the field. It slid to a halt with locked wheels, almost too close for comfort.

He handed me the bottle and the equipment.

'I think it's all here.'

'Good. We'll give it to her now, before we mess her about anymore. We'll drip it into her slowly. You can hold the bottle while I get on with the job at the other end.' Using the binder twine to bring up the jugular vein, I inserted a wide-bore intravenous needle, connected the rubber tubing and left him holding the bottle. I adjusted a clamp to regulate the flow and returned to the business end of the heifer.

The anaesthetic had taken effect. The tail was limp and lifeless. Once more, I washed and lubricated my hands, sank on to my knees and started to push the remains of the calf back inside the heifer. Feeling nothing, she no longer resented or resisted my efforts. It took a few minutes to find the front legs and bring them up into the pelvis. I attached calving ropes to each leg and handed them to the cowman.

'We've got to do all the work now. Having had that spinal anaesthetic, she's not going to give us any help herself. Not that she'd give us much anyway, in her state. You pull both ropes. I'll stay inside for the time being and guide the stump of the neck. There's some sharp pieces of bone sticking out where it was cut through. They may get caught up and tear her.'

Being an Angus cross-half, it was nice and small. It didn't take too much pulling to get the shoulders out even though it was pretty dry. The rest followed easily. The afterbirth had already separated. After cleaning myself, I lit up and leant against the trailer watching the level of glucose saline in the bottle. When it was empty, I took over, disconnected the tubing and pulled out the needle.

We rolled her up on to her brisket. She was too weak to hold herself and she sagged back on to the grass. We pulled her up again and used the two straw bales from the trailer to prop her up.

'Leave her one of these buckets with clean water. When you come up to feed the others this afternoon, you could bring her up a few armfuls of good hay. Don't worry about trying to get her to stand up today. She's had a pretty tough time. If she's not up by tomorrow morning, give us a ring. If she is up, I should bring the whole bunch of them back, handy to the dairy. Let her walk down quietly with them. You needn't milk her out till then. She won't have much for a few days after going through this lot.'

We hitched the trailer back on to the tractor and drove back to the farm.

On my arrival at the surgery, I was met by Mike.

'Two things,' he said. 'A Mrs Something hyphen-Smith has been ringing up all morning. She said you promised to go and see her peke and where were you. And a Mrs Turner from Manor Farm, called in about an hour ago. She was hopping mad.'

'What was she annoyed about? I only asked her to drop in a urine sample from one of their cows; I think it might have kidney trouble.'

'Well, her husband, after a lot of hanging around, managed to collect a decent sample. She was coming into town to do some shopping so she brought it with her. She put it in the handle-bar basket of her bicycle. On the way here, she went into a shop. When she came out, the urine sample was missing. Unfortunately they'd put it into a Gordon's Gin bottle! The Turners are going to try again and use a lemonade bottle next time. You'd better ring up Mrs hyphen-Smith right away and still her heaving bosom.'

'All right. I'll ring her and go and see her now.'

The tyres of my car crunched on the expansive sweep of gravelled driveway. I drove round the lawn with its wide-spreading cedar tree and stopped in front of the imposing portal which had originally been designed to accommodate horse-drawn carriages. Carrying my black leather case, I walked up the steps and pulled a well-polished brass knob. In the bowels of the house, a bell tolled. I was kept waiting. The door was then opened by a prim and middle-aged maidservant in stiffly starched cap and apron. She gave me an unfriendly stare and her eyes travelled to the case I was carrying.

'Madame is too busy to see anybody and commercial travellers are expected to use the tradesmen's entrance.'

She started to close the door. Using the best salesmen's technique, I advanced one foot into the doorway and gave her what I hoped was a winning smile. The door continued to close.

'I believe Madame is expecting me. I'm the vet.'

The maid raised one hand to her mouth and swiftly re-opened the door.

'I'm ever so sorry, sir. I didn't think you was the vet. Please come in, I'm sure. I'll tell Madame you're here.'

She bustled off, leaving me standing in the hall. I was then shown into the lounge—an ornate, over-furnished room with a hint of mothballs in the stuffy atmosphere.

Madame bore down on me and ordered me to sit down. I sat and looked across the room at the two pekes. From their cushions, they looked back at me with disdain.

'I'd like you to examine Pansy as well as Po.'

'What seems to be the matter with Pansy?'

'Oh. There's nothing wrong but I thought it would be nice if you looked at her. She gets upset if Po gets all the attention.'

I looked around me.

'Where shall we examine them? Do you have a table in here I can use? Or shall we use the kitchen table?'

'Oh no. I couldn't let them go on the kitchen table. It's much too cold and hard. They wouldn't like that at all. I'll put their cushions on this occasional table. You can examine them in here.'

'We'll look at Pansy first. I'll go and get my stethoscope from the car.'

On my return, Pansy was already enthroned on her cushion. I offered her the back of my hand. She took a quick, yapping bite at it and missed.

Madame wagged one finger at her.

'That's naughty. You mustn't bite the nice man. He's trying to help you.'

'What did you want me to examine her for? Are you worried about anything in particular?'

'I just wanted to know if she's all right.'

'She looks all right to me,' I answered lamely.

'But I'd like you to give her a thorough examination.'

'She's not off her food. Is she?'

'Oh no. She eats all right. She likes me to feed her, of course. I hand her a little piece and talk to her nicely and then she takes it. Then I hand her another piece. She's very good really and she loves her chocolates in the morning. She always has two at eleven o'clock. Sometimes I'm naughty and let her have three. They have to be soft-centres. I call them her elevenses and at tea-time she has a sweet biscuit.'

'How interesting,' I commented, reaching for my stethoscope. 'Perhaps you could steady her head while I listen to her heart.'

I placed the head of the stethoscope against the bitch's chest wall, just behind the left elbow. The heart sounds were inaudible, being masked by a continuous rumbling growl from the bitch.

'That seems all in order,' I announced firmly.

'Would you like to look at her dewclaws. She caught one of them in my cardigan last week. I nearly called you out, I was quite worried at the time.'

I moved my hand to pick up her front paw. With remarkable speed, she bit me on the thumb. I jerked my hand away and stood nursing it.

'Isn't she naughty? If you're going to behave like that Pansy, you won't get your biscuit this evening.'

I was approaching the end of my nervous tether.

'If you want me to give her a thorough examination, I think it would be better if you brought her to the surgery. You could bring Po too. They'll keep each other company.'

'I was hoping that you'd examine them both here. They hate going to the surgery.'

I had a sore thumb and was adamant.

'I think they must come to the surgery. We have all the facilities there. If necessary we can X-ray them.'

'Oh yes. I'd love to have them X-rayed. It was only last week I was talking to Lady Brown. She'd just had her little Yo-Yo X-rayed.'

'I'll phone you tomorrow to make the appointment. Now I'll go and wash my hands, if I may.'

On the way back to the surgery, I examined my injured thumb more closely. It was throbbing fiercely in time with my pulse rate. The skin had been punctured in two places by the

100

bitch's dirty little canine teeth, not deeply, but there was considerable bruising. It felt very tender.

At the surgery, I dressed the wounds and covered them with sticking plaster. I was offered a cup of tea but no sympathy by the surgery girls. I explained what had happened and was told I should be more careful. Anyway, I shouldn't call the dear little peke nasty names. I was a veterinary surgeon and I was supposed to love little doggies.

CHAPTER TWELVE

SAMBO THE MONKEY

You'd think it was the easiest thing in the world to get a dog and a bitch to mate. It happens often enough when you don't want it to.

This owner—there are many in the dog-breeding fraternity —wanted to confuse nature by breeding down in size. She had a large bitch, and without any consideration for the bitch's feelings, she had chosen a small dog to be the sire.

I was called, in a professional capacity, to assist.

Though physically incompatible, the dog and the bitch were willing. I was to be 'best man'.

The back garden of the house afforded greater privacy than the front, which only had a low wall to separate it from the public foot-path which carried a heavy volume of school-boy traffic. The back garden also had the advantage of a sloping lawn.

We gave them their first introduction on this lawn.

The bitch, either from impatience or misplaced enthusiasm, kept turning round, which put her short-legged bridegroom at an even greater disadvantage.

Our next attempt was on a short flight of steps leading down from the lawn. The bitch moved forward and he fell off.

A small wooden box was provided and placed in a suitable position. This again was a failure, one short and ecstatic rhumba movement of her rear end and one of his feet slipped off the box.

Eventually, with the panting owner holding on to the bitch's head, I took hold of the dog's two hind legs and lifted him into position. Success appeared to be imminent, but after several minutes my arms were tired and aching. Though he appeared to be capable of sustaining the pace, I was not. To relieve my arms of the tension, I kneeled down carefully, not wishing to distract him. He took my change of posture in his stride. I remained in the kneeling position, holding a paw in each hand to stop them slipping off my thighs and bent forward over their backs. I felt as though I was taking an active part in the production of a canine 'blue' film. My embarrassment was not lessened by an audience of several village dogs watching the proceedings avidly from the other side of the garden fence.

The climax of my embarrassment came when the bitch turned her head to one side and looked at the dog with apparent indifference. She then turned her head to the other side, looked me in the eye and, with gentle affection, gave me a long wet lick across the face.

One of the easiest and most frequently practised operations is the spaying of young, immature female cats.

It is a total hysterectomy, involving the removal of the uterus and both ovaries. The head surgery girl had admitted a kitten. Her name was Lizzie. She was a tabby with big bat-like ears.

I anaesthetised her with intravenous pentothal and clipped and shaved a square area on her left flank. After sterilising the skin and scrubbing up, I clipped sterile cloths around the operation site. Using a small, sharp-bladed scalpel, I incised the skin and muscle layers to open up the abdominal cavity. The uterus, no thicker than a match in a small kitten, lay under the lumbar fat. I searched for it, using slender pointed forceps, without success. I enlarged the incision and searched again. After a further five minutes probing, I stopped and checked that I had made the incision in the right place. Everything seemed to be in order so I continued the search. It was hot in the operating room and beads of sweat were trickling down my nose. The surgery girl wiped my face with a hand towel and lightly chided me for having lost my touch. I put out my tongue to her and continued the search. Several minutes later, I laid aside the forceps.

'It must have been born without a uterus or it's already been spayed.' I paused and looked at the surgery girl.

'By the way, did you check it when it came in?'

She looked at me for several seconds, bit her lower lip and slowly shook her head.

Lifting up one of the sterile cloths, I folded it forward.

'Pull its tail out of the way.'

The girl did as she was told and I peered underneath. I grinned.

'Who's losing whose touch? This kitten happens to be a male. A tom kitty. I know because I can count up to two.'

'I'm terribly sorry. I always look to make sure when they come in, but a whole lot of people arrived at once this morning. This woman hadn't made an appointment, she was in a hurry and she kept calling it "she". I'm afraid I forgot to check it. What shall we do?'

'The first thing we'll do is stitch up this bloody great hole I've just made. The next thing we'll do is castrate it.'

'I mean, what shall we tell the owner?'

'We have a choice. We can charge her one guinea for a castration or two and a half guineas for a spay. She'd probably never find out that it wasn't a female.'

'You can't do that. You'll have to tell her we made a mistake.'

'There's another alternative. I once heard of a similar case. The owner was told a cock-and-bull story about the cat being a rig, that is, only having one descended testicle, the other one being in the abdominal cavity. It was explained that the incision in the flank was necessary to remove it. She was only charged five guineas and was well pleased. She gained a lot of satisfaction telling all her friends about her cat's involved operation.'

It was a male, South American Woolley monkey, with a long prehensile tail and not very attractive habits.

When it was young, the owners were entertained by its quaint little ways and were therefore more tolerant of its misdemeanours. It had a spacious cage, hung on the wall in the kitchen—it being the warmest room in the house. From this vantage point, it used to pee on the Aga stove and was fascinated by the hissing on the hot-plate.

The cats, one Burmese, one Abyssinian and a seal-point Siamese, were not amused by this intruder in their private domain. They viewed with disdain their owners' obsession with this new toy. It was, no doubt, the passing whim of mere humans to have fallen for the dubious charms of this hairy primate. They were smugly confident that the novelty would soon wear off.

In their opinion, his image became tarnished when he diverted his attention from the hot-plate of the Aga to their regal selves, lying in soporific splendour against the warm side of the stove.

The impact of the first spray of monkey urine was not fully appreciated and their reaction was confined to a rapid flicking of the ears. As the monkey, with practice, improved his aim, their position became untenable. Their withdrawal was controlled and executed with studied indifference.

One day, as they had perhaps expected and certainly hoped, this moron of a monkey went too far.

The old vicarage was next door. The incumbent and his young wife were frequent visitors to the house of the monkey. The wife was meek, mild and unworldly; from stock of several generations of bible-punchers.

The harsh rattle on the bars of the cage interrupted the tranquillity of the warm kitchen and diverted the attention of the occupants from their game of Scrabble.

The monkey owner's wife was the first to look up and take notice. She pretended to ignore it and gazed steadfastly at her row of seven letters. The vicar's wife was next. She averted her eyes but was, thereafter, unable to concentrate on the game in hand.

In the first full flush of adolescent youth, this unattractive anthropoid had a massive erection. He was amusing himself with it on the bars of his cage, as small boys do with a wooden stick along the railings of a park. As neither the vicar nor his wife was able to give undivided attention to the game of Scrabble, it was abandoned and they took their leave.

The monkey and his cage were moved next day into the cold sitting-room and the cats resumed their cherished position by the Aga.

It was some years later that Sambo developed the full and dangerous potential of his adult canine teeth. They were long, very sharp and were designed by nature for aggression. Sambo was becoming aware of his superior armament. His owner was also aware of them. Sensing his owner's cautiousness, Sambo began to appreciate that the balance of power had shifted and was now, he thought, marginally in his favour. To confirm his ascendency, he frequently displayed his new weapons and occasionally made use of them.

An angry monkey in a padlocked cage was presented to me in the surgery one morning by the owner with a heavily bandaged hand. His request, accompanied by a nod of his head in the direction of the cage, was that I 'did something about it'.

I asked him what he wanted 'done about it'.

'If you can't make him better behaved, you'd better put him to sleep.'

I pointed out that it would be better to disarm him by removing his upper and lower canine teeth.

As I looked at the monkey, shivering with impotent rage in his padlocked cage, my mind went back to student days and an occasion when a large and equally aggressive chimpanzee was brought into the Veterinary College. It was attended by two of the keepers from the nearby Zoo and was apparently suffering from toothache. The plan of campaign had already been drawn up. The crate in which the chimp was incarcerated was airtight except for a wire grill which could be occluded and a small-bore pipe let into one side of the box.

The door over the grill was shut and a rubber tube was connected on to the pipe. Several large bottles of ether were available and, with the aid of a foot pump, a mixture of air and ether was pumped into the crate. There was a glass panel in the top through which the chimp could be viewed and the degree of anaesthesia assessed.

The pump was operated with enthusiasm by the two keepers

working in rotation. The air in the room became filled with the heavy, sickly odour of ether. The rate of pumping slackened off appreciably as the two keepers inhaled more and more ether. The chimpanzee, viewed through the glass, was apparently unaffected. He sat there, looking back at them through the glass panel. One of the keepers thought that he winked at him but it may have been an ether-induced hallucination. As they became progressively more incapable of pumping, two students were ordered to volunteer to carry on the work. They also became affected by the fumes and their plight was noted by the professor of Veterinary Surgery.

He decided to carry out a personal inspection and weaved his way through the ether laden atmosphere to peer through the glass inspection panel. The chimp was sitting happily and unaffected by the fumes with one thumb pressed firmly over the inlet end of the pipe, so that the only space in the building which was free of ether fumes was the inside of his snug little box.

I looked at Sambo, still chattering with rage at the indignity of being confined in a small cage and being stared at by total strangers. It was bad enough having been tricked into entering this prefabricated prison by the transparent ploy of a banana. Any young monkey worth his peanuts would have ignored it. It was now becoming intolerable, after a harrowing journey in the back of a car and the insulting inquisition of a gaggle of humans. His anger though was tempered with apprehension. He had an uneasy feeling that the future boded ill for him.

The door of his cage was unlocked, opened a fraction and a large angling net introduced. It swooped down on him. He fought bitterly, teeth and nails, but became hopelessly entangled. Chattering shrilly, he was drawn out of the cage. As fear overcame anger, he fell quiet and eyed his captors with anxiety and reproach. With short ceremony, a dose of tranquilliser was injected into the muscles of his bottom. He was then left to spit and glare at his tormentors until the injection took effect.

After twenty minutes, the transformation in his demeanour

was little short of miraculous. He became docile and trusting. He had escaped from the entanglements of the net and was sitting at the back of the cage. I opened the door and introduced my hand with index finger extended. A small clammy hand grasped it, seeking comfort and reassurance.

I led him gently from the cage and sat him on the surgery table. With complete submission, he allowed me to open his mouth and inspect his vicious looking canine teeth.

Using a dental syringe, I blocked off the area around each tooth with local anaesthetic. He continued to sit quietly on the table, holding hands with his owner.

Sambo showed neither reaction nor resentment to the pricking of the needle. By the time I had finished the last tooth, the first one was already insensitive. The roots of the canine teeth were considerably bigger than the exposed crowns, as with the tip of an iceberg.

To extract them, it was necessary to cut away a flap of the gum and then chisel away the underlying section of the jawbone to expose the side of the root. The complete tooth, root and crown were than levered out sideways. All four canines were treated in a similar fashion and the flaps of the gum sutured back into position using fine catgut.

The following day the effects of the tranquilliser had worn off. Sambo was once more his normal, unpleasant, aggressive self. His mind was occupied with his four gaps, which he explored continually with his tongue and intermittently with his finger-tips. He could however still raise a supercilious snarl when approached by his once loving owners. These visual threats now carried less authority. Sambo was nonplussed at the indifference shown to his warnings. Only yesterday they were bowing to his superiority.

His cage door was opened and a hand introduced. This intrusion on his privacy hadn't taken place since the days when he was a timid youth. He flew at it with an angry chatter and received a cuff on the ear for his pains. He retreated, dumbfounded that they had the temerity not only to question his superiority but to retaliate and actually chastise him.

CHAPTER THIRTEEN

A PREGNANT POODLE

MRS MATTHEWS was an influential breeder and judge of miniature and toy poodles. She had set views on the subject of dogs and veterinary surgeons and felt that she was qualified to voice her opinions on both.

I had spoken to her on the phone on previous occasions when she had informed me that she wished to speak to one of the partners; preferably the senior one. Veterinary surgeons, however well qualified, who were not partners, were in her order of things bracketed bottom with office boys and plumbers' mates.

She rang up one evening when I was on duty and took it as a personal affront that neither Bill nor Mike was available.

One of her bitches, a very valuable champion toy poodle, had been trying to whelp all afternoon without success. She had, of course, diagnosed the trouble, and was kind enough to tell me that I would have to do a caesar. She regretted that it had to be me, but realised that she had no other choice.

She brought the bitch over to the surgery and I examined her. To my annoyance, she was, of course, right. A caesarian was necessary. As neither partner was available, she told me that she would stay and supervise the operation. With rare courage, I told her she would not. Both partners, I stated falsely, had decreed that no owner was allowed to watch an operation. With obvious misgivings, she left her precious bitch in my rude hands and departed in a frosty silence.

I prepared a steriliser with the necessary instruments and swabs. While it was boiling, I rang the head surgery girl, to get her to come and help. She was out and her mother didn't know where. The other surgery girl was also out. The instruments were still boiling when Mrs Matthews rang up to ask how her bitch was getting on. She made it quite clear that she expected me to have finished the operation. I was obviously grossly incompetent.

It was virtually impossible to carry out a caesar, under aseptic conditions, without assistance. There would be great risk to the bitch and with no one to resuscitate the puppies, only a slim chance of their surviving.

I rang Anne. She agreed to help but didn't think she'd be much use, as she'd never done anything like that before.

With her assistance in holding the bitch steady and bringing up the vein on its foreleg, I anaesthetised her lightly with pentothal. She then held open the bitch's mouth and pulled the tongue well forward, while I pushed a rubber tube down its wind-pipe. This tube was connected on to the anaesthetic trolley which supplied a controlled flow of oxygen, nitrous oxide and ether.

'What are you doing that for?' asked Anne. 'Why don't you just use the injection to keep her under?'

'Because I want live puppies if possible and they don't tolerate pentothal very well. Once they're removed from Mum here, they'll be on their own as regards eliminating and coming round from the anaesthetic. They do this far more easily with nitrous oxide and ether than they do with pentothal.'

'How do you know the puppies are alive anyway?'

'Because I listened to their heart-beats with a stethoscope.'

'Could I have a listen?'

I passed her the stethoscope and held the chest-piece or diaphragm against the bitch's distended abdomen.

'I can't hear anything,' she said, screwing up her face. 'What should they sound like?'

'Like a watch ticking. Quite fast. Much faster than the bitch's heart.'

I moved the stethoscope until it was over the bitch's heart.

'Can you hear that?'

'Yes. I can hear that all right. Does my heart sound like that?'

'Yours will be slower, considerably slower than that, with a more distinctive double sound. Like "lub-dub".'

I clipped, shaved and sterilised an area of skin, scrubbed my hands and finger-nails with antiseptic soap and clipped the sterile operating cloths around the operation site.

'When I get the first puppy out, I shall throw it at you. I want you to rub it briskly with that towel to dry it and induce it to start breathing. Once it starts squeaking, lay it in that box with the electric heating pad.'

I picked up a scalpel from the steriliser, felt the bitch's skin with my fingers and made a sweeping incision. One small artery spurted blood across the table. I clamped it off and swabbed the area clean. As I started to cut through the muscle layers, I looked across at Anne. She yawned and there were small beads of perspiration on her forehead and upper lip.

'Sit down on the floor for a minute,' I told her.

'Why?' she asked.

'Don't bloody argue. Do as I say.'

She looked peeved but did as she was told. I smiled down at her.

'That's better. You've got more colour now. You were on the point of fainting and if you'd gone crashing down on this hard floor, you might have hurt yourself. Anyway, I need your help and you wouldn't be much use to me lying flat on your back.'

She produced a wan little smile.

'I was feeling a bit funny. It's very hot in here and I don't like the smell of the ether. I don't mind the sight of blood but I didn't like it when you cut through the skin and it gaped open.'

'You'll get used to it in time and it's nothing to be ashamed of. When it comes to blood, injuries or operations girls are usually tougher than men. We get more men passing out cold in the surgery than women. When you feel better, stand up. If you feel funny again, sit down at once and rest your head on your knees.'

I continued cutting through the muscle layers until the abdomen was open, then felt around inside with two fingers. I located the gravid uterus and very, very gently eased it up and out through the incision.

111

Anne was back on her feet and watching me.

'I shall want your help now. Get the towel and be ready to take a puppy from me.'

I packed gauze swabs all round the exposed uterus, so that any fluid which escaped when I incised it would be absorbed and would not run back into the abdominal cavity.

A quick cut through the wall of the uterus and a puppy's head bulged out, covered in foetal membranes. Using whelping forceps, I grasped the head and eased the whole puppy out, stripped off the membranes and broke the umbilical cord. Its heart was beating well.

'You're on your own now chum,' I said to it and held it up for Anne to see.

'Hold out your hands with the towel across them.'

I dropped the puppy on to the towel.

'Now give it a good rubbing. Don't be afraid to rub too hard. They're as tough as old boots. Keep at it until it starts squeaking.'

With something to occupy her, Anne looked much better and was beginning to enjoy herself.

'What are you doing now?' she asked.

'Taking out the afterbirth. Each puppy has its own, it's fairly intimately attached to the uterine wall and if I'm too rough with it, it might tear or cause a lot of bleeding. How are you doing with junior there?'

'All right. I think it just gave a little squeak. Listen.'

It lay flat and limp on the towel, giving sporadic gasps.

'Give it another brisk rub, then open its mouth and blow down it.'

She did as she was told. After a few moments it uttered a thin cry.

'Good show. Keep up the good work. There'll be another one coming shortly, so stick that one in the heated box.'

Squeezing the uterine horn, I gradually worked another puppy down towards the incision, pulled it out, hind legs first this time and tossed it across to Anne.

After removing the third puppy and its afterbirth, I sutured the incision in the uterus, removed and counted the swabs and replaced the uterus in the abdomen. The muscle incisions were closed with catgut and the skin with braided nylon.

'There we are,' I said, removing the sterile cloths from around the wound. 'That should keep the draught out. How are you getting on with your triplets?'

'Two are fine. The one you pulled out backwards hasn't started squeaking yet. Doesn't look very lively to me.'

I picked it out of the box, pursed my lips round its mouth and nostrils, then blew and sucked gently to clear any mucus from its air-passages. Three or four brisk rubs—much more vigorous than those administered by Anne—started it squeaking plaintively.

The bitch, very highly anaesthetised throughout the operation, was beginning to come round. She was coughing and trying to chew the tracheal tube. I pulled it out and wrapped her up in a blanket, leaving her puppies on their heated pad until she was sufficiently conscious to appreciate them.

Anne was standing watching the bitch when I returned from phoning the owner.

'She seems to be straining a lot. Is that normal?'

'She's only half conscious. Nobody's told her that she's had a caesar and she probably thinks that she's still got to produce them herself.' I said this with confidence. As I continued to watch the bitch, my confidence waned considerably. She was straining hard and at regular intervals.

I moved the blanket and peered at her rear end. A bulge of foetal membranes was protruding through the vulva—yet I thought I'd removed them all during the operation. I popped the bulge with my finger nails and a clear fluid out. A few strains later and a small black nose appeared. The doorbell rang.

'That'll be Mrs Matthews,' I said to Anne, with the edge of panic in my voice. 'Stall her off. Shove her in the waiting room. Tell her I'm just cleaning up the bitch. Tell her anything.'

The puppy's head was not far enough out to get a good grip on it. It was wet and kept slipping out of my fingers. Several strains and many long seconds later, I was able to get my fingers round the back of its head. The operating room door opened and Mrs Matthews strode in. Her voice cut across the room.

'She's all right, I hope.'

I remained kneeling over the bitch with my back to her.

'Yes. She's all right. I'm just cleaning her up. She's got quite a bit of stuff coming out of the vagina. Anne—will you get a large lump of cotton-wool.' I had the puppy's head and thorax in my hand. Only the hind quarters and the afterbirth remained. They followed quickly, masked from view by the large lump of cotton-wool. I concealed the whole soggy mass in my hand, stood up, and as I turned round to face the owner, slipped my hand nonchalantly into my trouser pocket.

'You may take her home now. Watch her with the puppies. She may not recognise them as her own at first. Keep them warm and——'

'That's all right,' she interrupted. 'I've had a lot of experience. You don't have to tell me anything.'

After she had left, Anne helped me clean up the instruments.

'Why did you leave that last puppy in her? Why didn't you take it out with the others?'

'Because I didn't know it was in there and didn't look. Inexcusable carelessness. It must have been right down in the body of the uterus—right inside the pelvis. I'll be bloody careful not to make that mistake again.'

'She managed to have that puppy on her own. Why did she need a caesar to remove the others?'

'She may have been able to have them on her own, but I was bullied into it by the owner. If it had been anybody else, I would have given her an injection of pituitrin, waited a bit and relied on my own judgement. But I've had cases where they've produced a puppy, even a live one, and then needed a caesar for the rest.'

'Was that last puppy alive?'

'No. But if it had been, I'd have sacrificed it, rather than try and explain it away to Mrs Matthews.'

'What did you do with it? I felt sure she'd see it.'

The lining of my pocket clung damply to my thigh. I pulled out the puppy, still attached to its greenish black afterbirth, which was adhering to a damp and greenish-black stained ten shilling note.

CHAPTER FOURTEEN

PROFESSIONAL JEALOUSY

THE front door bell rang at seven-thirty one morning. I let it ring. My landlady would answer it. It was her front door, not mine. I was off duty until surgery at nine. It rang again—insistently. She must have overslept—or perhaps she was dead. Reluctantly, I climbed out of bed, shrugged on a dressing gown and bumbled down the stairs.

Expecting to find the milkman or someone who wanted to read a meter, I eased it open, wincing as it squeaked, and peered blearily out into the ghastly light of day.

Anne, with her hair astray, stepped forward and grasped my hand.

'You must come and help me. My mare, Cherry. She's desperately ill. I'll leave my scooter here and come back with you in your car.'

'Why didn't you ring the surgery?' I asked. 'Mike's on duty. He'd have gone out and seen her. Or is he already out on a call?'

'I didn't know she was ill until I got to the stables at seven this morning.' She was on the verge of tears and weeping women used to upset me considerably. I held her hands to steady both of us and pulled her into the hall.

'Tell me more. What's happened?'

'Captain Henry found her down in her box at six o'clock this morning. She was rolling around in agony and lathered in sweat. Please hurry,' she pleaded.

'Hang on and I'll put some trousers on.' The panic was infectious. I left her in the hall, rushed up the stairs, got dressed and rushed down again.

I caught Anne by the hand and steered her towards the door. My landlady had, by now, woken up. She called to me

116

over the banisters as we were scurrying hand-in-hand through the front door. I'd have to explain everything to her later—and I knew she'd never believe me.

'Now. Tell me again what's happened,' I asked as we drove towards the stables. 'Why didn't Captain Henry ring through to the surgery?'

'You know he owes you a lot of money and he hasn't been able to pay off your bill for several months. Well, he didn't like to call the surgery—I suppose he was ashamed. He called another firm of vets.

'One of their new assistants was on duty and he came out. Captain Henry rang at six fifteen and he was at the stables at quarter to seven.'

'What's the problem then,' I asked.

She burst into tears, so I had to wait. We were nearly at the stables before she'd composed herself and was able to talk coherently.

'He'd been trying to stomach pump her for half-an-hour before I left. I couldn't bear it. She only shook her head once when he first tried to put the tube in. He hit her on the muzzle and swore at her. When she reared up again, he jerked her by the head-collar and called her a bitch. She's not a bitch. She's sweet and gentle and I love her. She's got an awful tummy-ache and she's not feeling well. Then he put a twitch on her and he screwed it up so tight that her nostrils were all twisted up and he couldn't get the tube in. That's when I left to come and get you. I'd watched you with that stallion at the Stud Farm and I was sure you'd be able to manage to stomach-tube her without putting on that dreadful twitch.'

I drew a deep breath and put my hand on her thigh.

'There's a thing called professional etiquette. I cannot possibly intervene or even comment—officially—if some other veterinary surgeon is dealing with a case. I wouldn't like it if some strange vet interfered with a case that I was treating.

'Captain Henry has called in this vet to look at a horse—the fact that it's your horse doesn't matter—he has been called in professionally, he is now in charge. If he is confident in his ability to treat it, he is entitled to carry on. If he is worried, then he can say so and call in a second opinion—one of his choice. I cannot possibly walk in to those stables and take over.'

'But you must, I want you to,' she insisted.

'All I can do, when we get there, is to ask him in a friendly way if he would like me to help him. If he says no, then there's nothing I can do. Either way, this is going to be very embarrassing. I should have turned you away from my doorstep as soon as you told me that some other vet was dealing with your mare.'

'What if he kills her?' she whimpered.

'He'll lose a client and his reputation will suffer.'

'You must do something.'

'I will. I'll talk to him, offer to help, reason with him—but it's still his case—not mine. If he refuses to accept my help, there's nothing I can do.'

I stopped the car in the stable yard and waited.

Captain Henry bustled out of a loose-box.

'Am I glad to see you,' he announced, forgetting his earlier infidelity in calling in a rival firm. 'This chap doesn't know a horse's nostril from its arse. For Christ's sake come and help.'

'I can't,' I announced. 'He's got to ask me.'

'I'll bloody tell him,' said Captain Henry.

'Better not to,' I said, feeling, in spite of my youth and relative inexperience, remarkably cool. 'Let me wander over and see what's happening.'

I wandered over, leaving them by the car, and looked over the loose-box door.

His hair was dishevelled and matted with perspiration. His loosened tie, shirt and face were liberally speckled with blood as were his hands and the stomach-tube. His face when he saw me registered surprise, then hostility. We had met before at local Veterinary Association meetings.

'What are you doing here?' he asked aggressively.

'Anne's a girl friend of mine,' I tried to explain. 'Can I help?'

'I'll manage,' he replied shortly. 'The bitch won't bloody well swallow.'

Anne had walked up behind me with Captain Henry.

'She's not a bitch and she's ill too,' she hissed defiantly.

The bloody face turned towards her.

'You can shut up and if I want any help, I'll ask for it.'

I took Captain Henry by the elbow and steered him back to my car.

'This is all very embarrassing, but Anne insisted that I came over here, I'd like to help, as a friend and for nothing, but what can I do?'

'I'm very sorry that I called him in, but you know how it is. I've had a couple of fairly brisk reminders from your boss. I didn't have the guts to ring him up at quarter past six this morning. This chap's been riding with Anne a few times and as it was her mare, I thought I'd call him in. Now I'm sorry I did.'

That evening, out of curiosity, I rang the stables.

'What happened to Anne's mare?' I asked.

'She's dead,' Captain Henry answered. 'Anne's at home and the doctor's given her some sedative tablets.'

'What happened?' I asked.

'He got the tube in eventually after a struggle and got Anne to do the pumping. She knew just what to do—she's a smart girl. When she'd finished pumping, she handed him the tube to blow down. He pulled the tube out and the mare started to cough and breathe heavily. The mare was very distressed. She went down on her knees, coughing and frothing from the nostrils then she died. The bastard had pushed the tube down into her lungs. What made it worse was that Anne had done the pumping. As soon as her mare collapsed and started to froth Anne seemed to know what had happened. If there'd been a pitch-fork handy, I think she'd have killed that vet.'

CHAPTER FIFTEEN

ODD CALLS

IT was after midnight before I got to bed. The telephone rang at 2.30 a.m. I felt as though I'd been asleep for only five minutes.

It was the wife of a well-known client, a pig farmer who kept about twenty Large White breeding sows.

Her voice was hushed and urgent.

'Can you come out at once. We've got some trouble here.'

Before I had time to wake up enough to question her, she had rung off. They were sensible clients—not given to calling us out unnecessarily and for them to ring up in the middle of the night, must mean a genuine emergency.

The farm house stood on the main road with a lane running down the side of it. The farrowing house, holding the breeding sows, and the sheds for the fattening pigs were two hundred yards down the lane. I had visited the farm several times before and knew my way around.

As I turned off the main road, it struck me as odd that the farm house was in total darkness. Normally on an emergency night call, the farmer and his family would be up, waiting about, and the building would be ablaze with lights.

I drove on down the lane. The farm buildings were also in darkness, except for a faint glimmer of light from the infra-red lamps in the farrowing house. Each pen in this house had a corner railed off against the sow. The piglets could creep off into this corner, lie under the warmth of the lamp and escape the danger of being trodden on or lain on by a clumsy sow.

The main fluorescent lighting was not switched on. Only the glow of the heating lamps showed through the windows which were opaque with dust and cobwebs.

As I stood by the car, pulling on my thigh boots, the only

sounds were the soft contented grunts of the sows and the occasional high-pitched, peevish squeal of a young piglet.

I still thought it was very odd that there was no sign of activity. I reasoned that it might be a nervous gilt, trying to farrow for the first time. They might have left the main lights off so that she and the other sows were not disturbed. Having rung me up, they could be sitting quietly watching her, waiting for me to turn up.

The door at the end of the building was ajar. I eased it open, looked inside and coughed quietly. The pig farmer's wife came up the central passage-way. Bedroom slippers and a blue nightie showed under the edge of a drab-coloured dressing gown. As she approached me, she held a finger up to her lips. She crept past me and carefully pulled the door shut.

'It must be an exceedingly nervous sow or gilt for them to take all these elaborate precautions,' I thought.

She took hold of me gently by the elbow and said 'Shush' again.

'Is your husband there?' I whispered, nodding towards the dimly lit far end of the building.

'No,' she whispered back. 'He's in bed. Asleep.'

'What's the trouble?' I whispered, feeling distinctly uneasy.

'It's the police,' she whispered back. 'I'm afraid they'll be here soon. I want you to stop them.'

'What are they coming for?' My whisper was now on a slightly higher note.

'Do you think it's wrong of me to wear red underwear?' she whispered.

I looked sharply at her and didn't reply. 'The neighbours have reported me to the police because I've been wearing red underwear,' she continued. 'Now the police are going to take me away. You've got to stop them. You must help me.'

'Is that why you called me out tonight?' I answered in an incredulous tone.

'Shush. Yes. I knew you'd be able to help. You go to the house next door to look at their dog. They're the ones who reported me to the police, I'm sure.'

I had known this woman for some time. She was a small-

121

boned, middle-aged person. She usually offered me a cup of tea when I visited the farm. I had often sat talking in the kitchen with her and her husband. He did most of the talking; normally, she was rather timid and self-effacing.

It was now my turn to take hold of her elbow, in an attempt to reassure her.

'I know the police well. We do a lot of work for them—helping them out in emergencies where animals are involved. I'll go back now and speak to them. They'll listen to me. Tomorrow morning I'll ring up your neighbours and tell them not to report you again. Now you go back to bed; quietly, so as not to wake your husband. You'll find everything will be all right tomorrow. I'll let you have two tablets so that you get a good night's sleep.'

I escorted her gently but firmly out of the farrowing house, into my car and drove her home. I gave her two tablets and waited for her to shut the back door before driving off.

Not far from the pig farm was a large area of woodland. The good timber had been sold off to a sawmill, leaving a few gaunt and spindly survivors towering uneasily over the brush-wood undergrowth of hazel and birch. Massive rain-filled ruts where the timber had been hauled out criss-crossed the land.

Squatting in part of this woodland was a family of gipsies. Not true Romany, as they had been static in this one area for several years and there had been a certain amount of out-breeding. They were not bad people but they had a bad name. Their crimes were petty; scrumping apples from orchards, filching a few potatoes or straw from farms, and the illicit grazing of their ponies. They were withdrawn, and resented strangers; strangers were usually farm bailiffs, policemen or council officials. They knew I was a vet and would stop me as I passed if they had trouble. They never rang or called at the surgery.

On this occasion, it was a pony with a massive, fly-blown, ulcerating sore on its shoulder and another on its withers, caused by overwork in an ill-fitting collar. One of the sons, aged about twenty, had stopped me. I invited him into the car and we drove down half a mile of rutted track to the encampment.

The pony was hobbled Irish or Arab fashion, with nine inches of cord joining its two forelegs above the fetlock joints. It would carry the scars round its shins for the rest of its weary years.

In spite of its considerable handicap, it was remarkably agile. It could walk, turn and swing round on its hind legs, using the front ones as a prop.

I picked the maggots out of the wounds, cleaned and dressed them and left instructions, which I knew would be ignored, that it was not to have a collar on or be worked until they had healed.

The father, dressed as his son was, in tight black trousers, dirty white shirt and dusty black trilby hat, came down the caravan steps.

'If yer tell me 'ow much, we'll drop the money into yer termorrer.'

'It'll be a quid and I'll have it now.'

He looked at me with black, gimlet eyes.

'Orl right then. You better come in.' He turned his head towards the caravan. 'I want yer t'see the missus anyway.'

I followed him up the four steps on to the tail-board and into the caravan. It was bright and clean inside, with a well polished oil lamp hanging from the roof and colourful curtains round the windows, a contrast to the camp site outside, with the rusty tin cans and assorted, cringing dogs scavenging through heaps of potato peelings and other garbage.

He slid his hand under the mattress of one of the bunks and brought out a thick wad of notes, peeled one off and stuffed the rest back. He kept it in his hand.

'Come 'ere, Flo. It's the vet,' he shouted through a partition.

She had an asiatic face, high cheek bones and dark eyes. Her greasy black hair was drawn tightly back from her forehead and tied to the nape of her neck. A large bosom was inadequately laced into a white embroidered bodice.

'Undo yer top and let him 'ave a look,' he ordered.

'Never did think much o' doctors,' he said to me. 'And there's not a good one round 'ere. I reckon you vets know much more. She's 'ad this lump on one of 'er tits for a long time now and it's beginning ter worry 'er. Av a go and see what you think. Come on Flo, 'urry up, 'e ain't got all day.'

Flo undid the lacing and flopped out one enormous bosom, taking some of the weight with her cupped hand.

Apart from the black and wrinkled nipple, it was glistening white with a fine network of purple veins. It was a strange contrast with the berry-brown hand and the sallow skin of her face.

'She's 'ad this lump, right deep inside it for some time now and it's got quite a bit bigger of late. 'Ave a feel.'

As I still hadn't got my pound note, I had a feel.

'What yer think, Doc?'

'It could be a cyst but it may be a growth. I think she ought to go to hospital and have it removed.'

'Don't 'old with them places. Thanks anyway.' He ushered me to the door.

'I'll take that pound note now,' I prompted. He handed it over reluctantly and I went down the steps.

Another deviation from the normal routine of veterinary practice occurred some time later.

It was nearly midnight when the phone rang. It was a client who had been into the surgery with her white bull-terrier dog on one or two occasions; she was an attractive, artificial blonde, aged about thirty-five. She had a habit of resting her slim, well manicured hand lightly on my forearm when she was talking to me. She wore expensive clothes and jewellery.

She sounded agitated or slightly drunk.

'Can you come out at once? Buster seems to be in agony and he can't stand up.'

'When did this start?' I hedged, to give me time to collect my wits.

'Only just now. He was all right earlier this evening.'

It could have been a strangulated hernia or acute peritonitis. It could have been one of several things.

124

'Has he vomited?' I asked. There was no reply.

'Hello,' I said. 'Has he vomited?'

'I think so,' she answered vaguely. 'You will come out, won't you?'

The house was on the outskirts of a village four miles out of town. After driving for less than a mile, I was waved down by someone walking along the side of the road. As I slowed down, I saw that it was a policeman.

He walked round to my side of the car.

'Excuse me, sir. Would you mind giving me a lift?'

I told him to jump in. He had been on his way home off duty, had a flat tyre and found that the spare was also flat. He asked where I was going. He lived another two miles on past the house I was going to, so I offered to take him home first and visit the dog on my way back.

'If it's all the same to you, sir, I'll wait in the car while you attend to the dog. Perhaps you'd be good enough to run me home afterwards.'

It was an elegant Georgian house with the front door opening directly off the pavement. I parked the car in the garage drive at the side of the house, walked back with my case and stethoscope to the front door and rang the bell.

It was answered by vociferous barking and the rattle of claws on parquet flooring. The door swung open slowly.

'Come in,' said a soft voice from behind it.

She was wearing a loosely fastened housecoat and, as she bent forward to restrain her bumptious bull-terrier, it was apparent she was wearing nothing else.

'Is this the sick dog?' I enquired.

'He seems much better now. I feel terrible having called you out now that he's recovered. You will stay and have a drink won't you?'

She was standing very close to me and lightly brushed her hand up the front of my trousers.

'I'll go and shut Buster away then we can have a quiet drink together.'

'Don't you want me to examine him?' I asked, taking a step backwards.

125

'It hardly seems necessary now,' she answered in a low voice, taking a step forward. 'Come along upstairs. I keep the drink in my bedroom.'

'And your husband?' I queried defensively.

'He's away in town. He doesn't care anyway.'

'I think I'd better be going,' I said, taking another step backwards.

She shrugged the housecoat off her shoulders, let it fall to the floor and stepped out of it, towards me.

'Don't you want me?' she appealed, holding her arms out.

'You're very attractive,' I said, retreating again. 'But I must go home now.'

Her eyes narrowed and a look of petulant anger fixed itself on her face.

'If you don't make love to me, I shall ring the police and tell them you've tried to rape me. It'll be my word against yours.'

'You don't need to ring the police,' I answered quietly. 'There's one waiting in my car outside. Shall I ask him in?'

'I don't believe you.'

I picked up my case and stethoscope and walked towards the door.

'If you don't believe me, have a look in my car as I drive off.'

'Everything all right sir?' asked the policeman as I got into the car.

'Yes. Thank you. But it very nearly wasn't. I'm very glad you were waiting outside.'

'We had a bit of trouble at this house two years ago. A young doctor, new to the district. He said she called him out on a night visit; she said he called in uninvited and tried to rape her. He had to appear before the Disciplinary Committee of the Medical Council and was lucky to get away with it. So I thought it would be better if you dropped me home after your visit. We've warned all the doctors. If they get a night call from her, we've advised them to call at the station first and pick one of us up. I didn't think she'd try it out on a vet.'

CHAPTER SIXTEEN

A FRESH START

AFTER three years as an assistant, I felt it was time to start out on my own. There was a market town about thirty miles to the south. On my next weekend off duty, I decided to look around it and assess the possibilities.

Thirty miles was a good distance. Close enough to keep in touch with my previous employers, yet far enough away not to encroach on their practice and cause ill-will.

Before visiting any of the estate agents to enquire about suitable premises, I drove around the town to get the feel of the place and study its geography. I visited the market, the railway station and the main shopping area. Over a cup of coffee, I studied a map of the town, noting the residential areas.

Not being able to advertise my arrival or presence as a veterinary surgeon, it would be of considerable benefit if my premises were situated where they would catch the public eye. If they were tucked away down some side street, it would take much longer for me to become known.

For the small animal, cat and dog, side of the practice, shop premises would be suitable for adapting into a clinic. Professional etiquette demanded that advertising be restricted to a discreet brass plate carrying only name, qualifications and profession. People, however, tended to look in shop windows and if the window was empty, it aroused their curiosity. If the premises could be so arranged that the front of the shop was used as a waiting-room, my clients, sitting waiting with their pets would arouse more curiosity.

An important consideration was how to dispose of the bodies of animals which either by accident or design had died. A back entrance with parking space would be a definite asset in this respect. Having to carry the body of a large dog such as an Alsatian or a Great Dane across a busy pavement to my car or a waiting lorry might well cause offence, especially in hot weather.

I called on three estate agents and accumulated a sheaf of particulars of various desirable properties, most of which were neither suitable nor desirable.

During lunch, I shifted through the pile of foolscap sheets and eliminated all but six. These I visited and by so doing, narrowed the choice down to three, one of which was a fairly strong contender. It was a single fronted shop with a recessed doorway on one side of the window, in which was displayed a large urn containing a few tired lilies. Painted in large black lettering on the window was the word 'Undertaker'.

This was encouraging. It was unlikely that coffins, occupied or empty, would be carried out through the front door. There would certainly be access to the rear of the premises, with parking facilities for one or more hearses.

There appeared to be a flat over the undertakers, which would be convenient for me to live in at first. As the practice (hopefully) grew and prospered, it would be useful for an assistant or animal nurse.

Driving back home and thinking things over, I decided that the undertaker's was definitely for me. It would not involve any large capital expenditure and the seven years' lease would give me time to look around for better premises if my venture prospered. I might then buy a plot of land and build an up-to-date Animal Hospital.

I would have to break the news to Bill and Mike that I was going to leave them and start up on my own. It would be bad news for them. Not that I rated my ability any higher than the next assistant, but because I knew my way to all the farms and was accepted by most of the farmers and stockmen.

'What do you want to do a silly thing like that for?' said Bill, the senior partner, when I plucked up the courage to tell him. 'Mike and I have been talking about offering you a partnership. How about it?'

'If you and Mike were both old and doddering, I would

accept. As it is, I don't want to remain a third junior partner for the next fifteen or twenty years.'

'It can be pretty tough being in practice on your own. You'll be on duty twenty-four hours a day, seven days a week and that includes Christmas day and other holidays. If, through sickness or injury, you can't work, not only will you get no money but you'll lose your clients to other vets who can offer a better service. In partnership with us, you'll have regular time off and three weeks' holiday a year. Whether you're off work, sick or on holiday, the practice will still be earning you money. Think about it.'

I thought about it and decided to take the plunge and start on my own.

I was allowed a day off to inspect the interior of the new premises and fix up the lease.

The interior was sombre, as befitted a funeral parlour. A few coats of white paint would be needed to brighten it up.

I had to give a month's notice, so that they had time to get a replacement for me. During this month, I used all my spare time and some of theirs organising the decoration and equipment of my new premises. Headed notepaper, prescription pads and visiting cards needed careful selection.

The two rooms at the back were converted into a consulting room and operating theatre. I had a porthole window fitted into the adjoining door, so that the more inquisitive of my clients would be able to look through into the operating room and be suitably impressed by the stainless steel, adjustable operating table and the rest of the cold, clinical equipment. Across the glass-covered back yard were two other rooms. One had been the carpenter's workshop, and it would make a good kennel-room for post-operative recovery and in-patients. The other would be a drug store.

I got a builder to build four large kennels along one wall, with eight smaller ones for cats and small dogs on top. They were lined with white tiles and had electric heating elements built into the floors. It was an expensive alteration but I felt it was justified. Apart from impressing clients who came to view their pets, it would improve the chance of recovery in animals suffering from post-operative shock.

I visited the Ring o' Bells down the road and introduced myself to the landlord, who greeted me affably from behind his well-polished bar. His bold hound's-tooth check riding jacket was adorned with a gold watch chain, and his sideburns and moustache were luxuriant. I bought him a drink and told him I'd just started in practice up the road.

'We need a good vet here,' he said in a warm, gruff voice. 'There's an old boy who comes here every market day, when he doesn't forget, but it's difficult to get him out of the pub. When they do manage it, he's never sober enough to work.'

I handed him my card, and said: 'There's an old saying, you know: "He's a veterinary surgeon and his wife drinks too".'

He gave a rich chuckle, offered me a return drink, and held the card up to examine it.

'I'll put this up where the customers will see it. It might do you a bit of good.'

I told him, rather primly, that it was not allowed; it would be counted as advertising, and veterinary surgeons and other professional men were not allowed to advertise.

He stuck it into a glass behind the bar, which already held a collection of other cards, grown dog-eared and dusty with neglect.

'Seems bloody silly to me,' he said. 'How are people going to get to know about you?'

'By the recommendation of other people.'

'But you've got to start somewhere, haven't you?'

'That's why I came here. Now you know who I am and that I'm just up the road from you.'

An advertisement, under a box number, in the local weekly paper for a girl willing to assist in the surgery and help with operations produced fourteen replies. These all needed interviewing, and it was not an easy task.

The girl I selected was barely fifteen. She had had an inadequate education at a small village school, but she seemed to have a lot of commonsense. She had no experience but she was willing to learn and was not over-sentimental about animals.

Her father was a shepherd and some of his calm competence invested his daughter. Her name was Eileen. She had light brown hair, blue eyes and a small pointed nose. She was about five feet three inches, not yet fully developed, but with nice legs. She was a little shy, which was understandable for her first interview, but she had a pleasant manner.

Her mother came with her for the interview. She was a level-headed country woman with bright, kind eyes. She wanted to make sure that her daughter behaved herself at the interview. She also, I think, wanted to make sure that I intended to behave myself with her daughter. I told her that, for the first few months, while she was learning what to do, I would only pay her two pounds a week. As she improved, so would her salary. I couldn't afford to pay her any more at the beginning, but I didn't tell them this.

To show that my intentions were quite honourable, I asked if I could meet her father.

'He's down at the Spotted Cow most evenings after seven, but he's usually home by nine. The public bar of course. He likes his game of darts.'

'I'll drop in one evening and see him,' I said.

My flat above the surgery was sparsely furnished with second-hand junk. The instruments, equipment and drugs had cost far more than I had anticipated. There was no money left over to furnish it as I would have liked.

The following week I moved in, hung a printed card in the window showing the surgery hours and sat and waited.

I waited a week. Nobody came. My only consolation was that I was theoretically on holiday from my last job and was getting paid. Eileen spent her time dusting and mooning about unhappily. I think she had expected to be immersed in a frenzied atmosphere from the very beginning. She was obviously disappointed.

On the Sunday evening, I drove out three miles to Eileen's village. The public bar was hazy with smoke, warm with friendly subdued chatter. A game of darts was in progress.

The chatter ceased and I was eyed as a stranger as I went up to the bar and ordered a pint of bitter. I leant one elbow on

131

the bar and watched the half-dozen occupants watching me. I nodded my head to them, they nodded back and the game of darts was resumed.

The dartboard light was shielded by a scalloped metal shade. Errant darts had punctured it in many places. Tiny rays of light escaped, stabbing through the smokey air and patterning the low darkened ceiling.

The landlord with his glistening bald head, regulation collar-stud and striped shirt and braces, coughed lightly in my ear.

'You're new here, aren't you?'

'Yes. I've just started up in town. In South Street, near the Ring o' Bells. I'm a vet.'

'Oh. You'm the fellow Fred's young Eileen's started work with. I hear you're pretty quiet. Not too much work.'

'No work at all,' I answered, with a crooked smile. 'It takes time to get known. It's bound to be quiet at first.'

'Word'll soon get round, you know. We need a keen young vet around here. 'Arry over there, playing darts with Fred; 'e's the stockman at Manor Farm. 'E was asking about you this evening. 'E's got some trouble with 'is calves. Pneumonia 'e reckons. 'Ave a word with 'im when they've finished.'

I was well into my second pint before they'd finished their game. They came over to the bar and the landlord introduced me to Fred first and then Harry.

They both nodded and stood awkwardly, holding their empty pint pots.

'Have a drink,' I offered.

They accepted diffidently. They eyed me steadily, with no expression on their faces.

'I thought I'd meet you if I came here,' I started, addressing Fred. 'Tell Eileen she mustn't be too disappointed because there's no work yet. It won't be long before she's complaining of too much,' I added, optimistically.

They nodded their heads again. Conversation was going to be difficult. They were withdrawn and reserved, like true countrymen. Why should they exchange idle banter with a stranger?

The landlord came to my rescue.

132

''Arry. You were asking about Mr—Mr——.' He stopped and looked at me.

'Farrier,' I volunteered. 'Denis Farrier.'

'That's a good name for a vet. Can you shoe a horse?' He laughed uproariously at his own joke, but nobody else did.

'You said you were worried about those calves, 'Arry. Why don't you ask 'im now?'

Harry scuffed the wooden floor with the toe of his boot.

'It's not for me to call 'im in. It's up to the Master and you know 'ow mean 'e is. 'E'll let 'em all die afore 'e calls in the vet. I'll 'ave another go at him and see what 'e says.'

'What about your whippet then?' Eileen's father interrupted. 'Why don't you let 'im 'ave a look at that?'

'' 'E can if 'e likes. If 'e's not too busy.'

'What seems to be the trouble?' I prompted gently.

Harry took a swig of beer before replying.

'It's not really mine. It belongs to Little Willie, our boy. 'E went after a rabbit this morning. It was on rough going, the rabbit jinked and 'e took a nasty tumble. The boy thinks 'e's 'urt 'is back.'

'If you want me to have a look at him, I will,' I said, not wishing to sound too keen. 'Do you live near here?'

When I was an assistant, I'd strongly resented anyone who wanted to talk 'shop' when I was off duty. It was different now. I was my own boss and was prepared to work for myself. As an assistant, I had worked hard when I had to, but I remained aloof from the life of the practice. It was not my practice. I was a salaried employee, earning money and gaining experience. I lived in a vacuum; unable or unwilling to appreciate my environment. In my own practice, I wanted to become involved; to integrate myself with the community. The public bar of a village inn was a good place to start.

'We're in the next cottage to Fred here. Just up the road.'

'When we've finished our beer, we could walk up and have a look at him,' I suggested.

Harry led the way up the garden path, round the side of the cottage to the back door. He introduced me to his wife, who was fussing over an old-fashioned, black-leaded kitchen range.

' 'E's come to look at Flash. Where's the boy?'

' 'E's down the garden. Feeding his rabbits. Flash is with 'im.'

We waited for Little Willie in awkward silence. For no good reason, I imagined him to be a school-boy, of about twelve or fourteen years.

He pushed his way through the door, with the whippet at his heels. He was over six foot two with a chest like a barrel. His khaki shirt was open to the waist showing a mat of hair. It was a late September evening and not too cold, but during the years that I knew him, even in the coldest weather, he dressed the same. He worked for the Rural District Council as a dustman and could carry two full dustbins, one in each hand. He treated his whippet with tender and loving care.

On this occasion, our first meeting, Flash had apparently recovered from her tumble. It wasn't necessary for me to examine her, but he insisted that I look at her. With loving care, he lifted her on to the kitchen table and proudly showed her off.

Some three years later, in the surgery, I had to break the news to him that his Flash had cancer of the liver and had no hope of survival. This massive hulk of a man, with his shirt still open to the navel, sat down on a chair and sobbed. He continued to weep; heaving sobs racking his solid body. What can you do with a weeping man? I couldn't hold his hand. I knew of no way to console him and I had several clients still waiting with their animals.

Eileen took over. She held one of his large, hairy paws in her two small hands and led him through to the operating room.

By the time surgery was over, he had recovered a little. We had hidden the stiffening remains of his beloved Flash. He stumbled out of the surgery alone.

Harry, Little Willie's dad, apologised for having bothered me unnecessarily, and by way of recompense took me back to the Spotted Cow for several pints of bitter.

CHAPTER SEVENTEEN

DOG ON A HOOK

THE second week was the same. Not a single client. My earlier feelings of depression were now more severe and were interspersed with moments of cold fear. Failure and the seven-year lease on the premises loomed ahead. The money spent on the conversion and the cat and the dog cages would be lost. The second-hand value of veterinary instruments was low.

On Sunday lunch-time, I decided to go down to the Ring o' Bells for a drink. As I walked out of the surgery door, a car pulled up. A man and his dog got out. The dog looked like a cross-bred beagle in shape, but it had spikey, gingery hair and a small moustache. The man's moustache was thin and black. He looked about thirty-five, wore a green pork-pie hat and a cream bow tie with large red spots.

'Are you the vet?' he asked. 'My name's Bob Ferguson. They told me down at the pub that there was a new vet, just started up here. Could you have a look at my dog?'

'Certainly,' I answered. 'Bring him in. What's the trouble?'

He smiled at me with a resigned air.

'I took him for a run along the river bank this morning. There were some men fishing from the bank and "nosey" here sneaks up behind one of them and helps himself to the bait. There must have been a spare hook and cast lying ready baited in the tin. When I called him back, I saw this cast hanging from his mouth. I pulled it but it wouldn't move. Do you think you could do something about it?'

'It might not be all that easy,' I told him. 'If you pulled it hard, the barb of the hook may have got stuck. We'll have a look and see what we can do. What's his name?'

'Pledger,' he answered.

'That's an odd name. Why call him that?'

'Well, his full name is Petty Officer George Pledger, but that's a bit long for everyday use. We only call him that on his birthday.'

'How did he get a name like that?' I asked.

'It was the name of a shipmate of mine. A good pal. He went down with his ship off Crete, during the war. He had gingery hair and a spikey moustache too.'

I stroked Pledger on the head and spoke to him before opening his mouth. The nylon strand with its little lead weights stretched out of sight over the back of the tongue. I inserted two fingers down his throat and depressed his tongue. He retched, but there was no sign of the hook. I let go, rinsed my hands and spoke to the owner.

'In most cases when a dog tries to eat a baited hook, it gets caught up on its lip or on the inside of its cheek. This is different. It's gone right down his throat. It may be in his stomach. The only way to find out is by an X-ray.'

'Where can I get him X-rayed?'

'I can take one now if you like,' I told him. 'It'll take about ten minutes to get the answer.'

'All right then. You'd better go ahead.'

I left him holding Pledger, went into the dark room and loaded an X-ray film into a cassette. I laid the dog on his side under the X-ray unit with the cassette under his neck and chest. The developed film showed the hook in startling clarity. It was well down the gullet at the point where it entered the chest. I called the owner into the darkroom and showed him the film.

'This is fairly serious,' I explained to him. 'There's no chance of either pulling it up or pushing it on down into his stomach. The only solution will be an operation called a pre-sternal oesophagotomy.'

'A what?'

'He'll need a general anaesthetic. I shall then remove the hook by cutting through the skin and muscle and opening up the oesophagus.'

'What are his chances of getting over it?'

'Fairly good, I should say. He'll be a bit sore afterwards.

You'll have to keep him on a liquid diet for several days.'

'What will happen if we leave it where it is?'

'He'll die.'

'Then you better carry on and do it. Will he have to stay the night?'

'If all goes well, he should be fit to go home this evening. Once he's come round from the anaesthetic, he'll be happier at home. He'll worry less if he's in familiar surroundings. Do you live far from here?'

'About three miles away,' he answered, handing me his visiting card. It described him as a representative for Farm Machinery.

'I'll ring you when I've finished to let you know how he's got on.'

'All right. I'll leave him with you now.' He patted his dog on the head. 'Best of luck old chap. You shouldn't go stealing fisherman's bait.'

As soon as the owner had left, I gave Pledger an injection of a tranquilliser, carried him through to the kennel room and shut him in a cage.

While the instruments and swabs were cooking in the steriliser, I rang through to Eileen. Luckily she was in and did not object to helping me; in fact she seemed very enthusiastic.

By the time I'd collected her and got back to the surgery, the instruments had cooled off. The sedative injection had taken effect. She carried the dog through to the operating room, crooning to him in baby talk. She placed him gently on the operating table.

'He looks awfully ill to me,' she commented.

'He's not all that bad. He's just doped by the injection I gave him half an hour ago.'

When he was anaesthetised, I strapped him on his back, then clipped, shaved and sterilised an extensive area of his neck. After scrubbing up and fixing the sterile cloths around the operation site, I incised the skin over the position, as indicated in the X-ray film, where the hook was lodged.

This was Eileen's first experience of an operation. I kept an eye on her to see how she reacted. She appeared to be calm and collected.

I dissected down until the oesophagus was in view and gently explored the area with a finger-tip. Feeling something hard, I withdrew my finger, swabbed the area free of blood and had a look. The black shaft of the hook was visible, curving out of sight. By careful dissection, I enlarged my field of vision. The hook had well and truly penetrated the oesophageal wall. The barbed tip had passed over and round both the vagus nerve and the carotid artery and was on the point of re-entering the wall again, having trapped both the artery and the nerve. I looked across at Eileen—she looked fine. Beads of sweat on my forehead were joining forces and trickling down my nose. I asked her to mop me up with a hand towel.

'Have you found the hook yet?' she asked.

'Yes. And he must have given it a helluva pull when he was trying to free it.'

I took a pair of artery forceps and clamped them on to the shaft of the fish-hook at the point where it curved over the artery, to hold it steady.

Lying in the steriliser was a pair of wire-cutters: ordinary electrician's wire-cutters. They looked out of place amid the shining, stainless-steel surgical instruments. Holding it steady with the forceps, I cut through the shaft of the hook. It was hard steel and took a lot of pressure on the cutters before it snapped. Holding on to the barbed and pointed end, I very gently eased it free and dropped it on the table.

Eileen picked it up and tested the point with her finger.

'It's sharp, isn't it,' she commented. 'I'm glad you've got it out.'

'That's only part of it,' I told her. 'You're going to remove the other half.

She looked at me with apprehension.

'How?'

'By pulling on that strand of nylon,' I answered, nodding my head towards the dog's mouth, from which the nylon cast with its lead weights was still protruding.

'Why do you want me to do it?' she asked.

'My hands are sterile, or should be. That strand of nylon

isn't. I want to remain sterile until I've finished stitching up.'

She nervously took hold of the loose end, as though it was going to bite her.

'Will it be all right if I just pull?'

'Go ahead and pull. There's no hook on it now.'

She pulled. After some initial resistance it came free. Still holding on to the end, she held it up in front of me, swinging it gently to and fro.

'Shall I throw it away?' she asked.

'No. We'll keep it to impress the owner.'

Eileen laughed and I knew she was going to make a good surgery girl.

I dressed the operation site with antibiotic powder and left it unsutured except for the skin incision which I closed with braided nylon. An infection which might have been carried through on the point of the fish-hook, if not controlled by the antibiotic powder, would have a free channel for drainage. If it did accumulate, I would only have to remove one or two skin sutures to let it out.

I carried Pledger, still unconscious back to the kennel-room, wrapped him in a blanket and switched on the under-floor heating.

At tea-time, when Bob Ferguson, the owner called, Pledger was still lying flat on his side, apparently unconscious. He spoke to him, calling his name. One eye opened and the blanket over his rear end slowly pulsed up and down as he tried to wag his tail.

'Wouldn't it be better to leave him here for the night?' he ventured. Pledger's pink tongue protruded hesitantly, curled at the tip. He tried to lick his nose, but was not co-ordinated enough to make contact.

'He's fit to travel home if you want to take him now.'

'I'd rather leave him here, if you don't mind. The kids would be very upset seeing him like this. He's their dog and they blame me for letting him swallow the hook.'

In the morning Pledger was standing up looking through the wire mesh of the cage door. He offered me a tentative wag of his tail, and accepted a drink of water. When his owner arrived, he gave a high-pitched whimper of delight. With a whiplash wagging of his tail, he tried to climb up the cage door. I opened it and he tumbled out. After rushing round in several tight circles, he clambered up his master's leg.

'He doesn't look any the worse for wear,' he said, happily. 'You'd hardly think he had an operation.'

I showed him the cast and the two pieces of the fish-hook.

'I'll keep that as a souvenir. When do you want to see him again?'

'Bring him back in ten days to have the skin stitches out. If you're worried about him, let me know. Don't give him any solid food for the next two days. After that he can have what he likes.'

'I'm at the market every week, selling agricultural machinery. Why don't you come along next market day. I can let you know how he is. I can also introduce you to several farmers.'

CHAPTER EIGHTEEN

THE HORSE'S MOUTH

MARKET day was on a Wednesday. It acted as the farmers' business forum, as well as their weekly entertainment and gossip centre.

When I had been an assistant to Bill and Mike, the practice had a retainer from the City corporation (Markets Committee) to attend. The City bye-laws stipulated that there had to be veterinary supervision, therefore one member of the practice had to attend. Apart from that, there were various farmers who apparently distrusted the postal system and preferred to pay their bills personally. The market afforded us the opportunity to collect.

It was also often necessary to act as arbitrator in any dispute that followed the sale of an animal. Was the thick and glutinous milk coming from a cow's udder merely colostrum, as she was newly calved, or had she got mastitis?

The prospective buyers had had ample opportunity to inspect the animals before they entered the sale-ring, but often they bought first and complained afterwards. The horse that they'd just had knocked down to them looked all right when it was trotted up by the dealer before going into the ring; now they weren't so sure. It seemed to be favouring its near-fore a little. On closer inspection, it now appeared that the wear on the front shoes was not quite even. The new owner would be disturbed by the thought that it might have a navicular disease. Though he had bid for it and bought it of his own free will, he was now reluctant to hand over the purchase price in the auctioneer's office.

An instant diagnosis would have to be made. This was not always easy, being surrounded by a throng of curious bystanders, in the presence of the disgruntled and suspicious purchaser and the belligerent horse dealer. The new owner might simply have had an attack of cold feet and wished to back out of his commitment. On the other hand his suspicions might be founded on fact. The time interval between first seeing the horse trotted up and seeing it again after the sale, might have been long enough for the effects of a local anaesthetic to have worn off. The dealer could have had the horse injected to mask the lameness prior to taking it to market. He might have merely given it a sharp rap with a hammer on its sound leg, so that for a short time the horse was not sure which leg to favour and went reasonably level. Any decision was bound to cause resentment by one party or the other, but if the diagnosis was accurate, the ensuing ill-will was short-lived and by next market day had been forgotten.

I went first to the dairy cattle sale ring, and sat high up at the back on the wooden tiered surround. The building was crowded. Not all those present were immediately connected with farming. There were school children, inquisitive holiday makers and various salesmen of insurance, patent medicines and farm fertilisers.

The atmosphere reminded me of a Spanish Bull-ring: the banked lines of spectators and the high wooden walls of the central, sawdust covered sale-ring. Cattle dealers and farmers, seriously intending to buy, lined the ring-side within eyebrow lifting distance of the auctioneer.

A bewildered Friesian heifer with a leggy three day old calf at her heels was driven into the ring. A rough-clad drover was behind her and kept her moving round to give the prospective purchasers a view of her from all angles.

The analogy with the bull-ring could be extended to include suffering: the mental torment of the heifer, evicted from the familiar surroundings of her home farm and the quiet intimacy of the loose-box in which, a brief three days earlier, she had borne her first calf; hustled with no explanation and little re-assurance into a cattle truck; goaded down the ramp into the market to follow, with mounting apprehension, her calf who was dragged, willy-nilly, with brave little bleating bellows, past lines of sweating fat-arsed cattle, to be tied up short in a vacant stall.

The heifer was sold and driven out of the ring, having to leave her calf who would be sold separately and to a different buyer.

The suffering was of a higher order than the short span of physical pain suffered by an enraged and bloody-minded Spanish bull. But there was no blood, no wounds and the traumatic effect on the heifer's nervous system was not seen, therefore it was not recognised as cruelty and was permitted in the name of trade.

I left the sale-ring and walked out of the building, past the pig pens with their bleeding-eared occupants—the fresh and neat round holes, punched through the skin and cartilage of the ear-flap indicated that they had been graded and that their owners would receive a guaranteed price. Then past fat, contented sows, indifferent to the squealing and suffering of their porcine neighbours. They lay on their sides in the straw, suckling a double row of eager little piglets, looking like the sausages which would probably be their ultimate destination.

In the central, open area, of the market was displayed the bright and brand-new agricultural machinery—the massive burnished three-furrow ploughs with their vivid blue paint-work. I thought back to the time on my uncle's farm when I had plodded behind a pair of huge, hairy-legged shires, guiding, not always as straight as my uncle would have wished, a rusty old single furrow plough. The breaking wave of the continuously turning sod had a mesmerizing effect on the ploughman. It induced tranquillity of mind. Being uncluttered, my brain was aware of every part of nature, even down to the small subterranean creatures so rudely disturbed by the single, shining, share.

Near the mechanical ploughs were the fire-engine red tractors, squatting powerfully on their fat, black tyres, canary yellow pick-up bailers and swathe turners. They contrasted spectacularly with the rusted, soil-encrusted second hand implements, offered for sale and lying, as though abandoned, nearby.

Leaning against the tailboard of a truck was Bob Ferguson,

my one and only client. His battered pork-pie hat and red spotted tie made him easily recognisable. He was talking earnestly to three men who looked like farmers. I didn't like to interrupt, so hung back and waited until the hoots of coarse laughter announced the end of his story.

His dog was in great form and he was well pleased. He introduced me to his friends and suggested that we went over the road to the Cattle Market Inn.

It was when I later returned to the market to collect my car, I was intercepted by one of the local horse dealers.

'I 'eard you was a vet,' he said.

He was a rough looking character with black and cunning eyes. He appeared to be suffering from a shortage of razor blades and coat buttons, the latter deficiency being made good with a frayed length of binder twine. He was pleased to meet me because he had a horse that was going thin and not feeding too well. I had the feeling that the welcome accorded was because I was a new face. He had probably exhausted his credit with all the other veterinary surgeons within visiting distance. I agreed to look at his horse and arranged to visit him the following morning.

The dealer's yard gave every indication from its contents that the owner did not confine his activities exclusively to horse dealing, but diversified to include second-hand cars and scrap metal.

I picked my way through the pot-holes, puddles and tangled wire and arrived at a line of decrepit stables. The dealer appeared from behind these stables, adjusting his dress with one hand and carefully squeezing the end off a half-smoked cigarette with the other. He gave me a brief nod, went into one of the boxes and led out a big-boned grey gelding on a rope halter.

It was in poor condition, with its ribs showing clearly. I asked him how old it was. He told me it was ten or eleven. I took off my jacket and hung it over the half door of the box, where I could keep an eye on it. I then spoke to the horse and stroked its muzzle before lifting its upper lip to look at its teeth. It was certainly over eighteen and probably over twenty years. He had not asked me to age it, so I refrained from comment. Sliding a hand gently into the sides of its mouth, I grasped its tongue and pulled it forward. Its molar teeth were irregularly worn. The third lower molar on the near side stood up more than half an inch above the rest. Its opposing number in the upper jaw was missing. I let go of the tongue.

'One of his upper teeth is missing,' I said. 'There's nothing for its opposite number to grind against and it's grown out of line. That's why he can't chew his food properly. If it's left much longer, he won't be able to eat at all.'

He gave me a look of suspicion and disbelief.

'I didn't know 'orses' teef kept on growing.'

'Well they do. Normally they wear down at about the same rate as they grow. When they get older, the front teeth don't wear down so much and they get longer in the tooth. That's how you can tell a horse's age,' I added pointedly.

'Can you do anything about the toof then?' he asked.

'It can be sheared off level with the others. That will only be a temporary measure because it will still continue to grow. The best way is to pull it out. He'll need a general anaesthetic to have that done. There's some risk in giving him an anaesthetic, in view of his age.'

The dealer was silent for a while, before replying.

'You better shear it off then. I shall be selling him in a few weeks, as soon as I can get some condition on 'im. I wouldn't want nothing to 'appen to 'im. Can you do it now?'

I told him that I hadn't got the instruments with me, but I could do it the following morning, if it was convenient.

''ow much is orl this going to cost me?'

'Three guineas, including the present visit and examination.'

'That's a bit steep, in'it?'

I pointed out to him that if he didn't have it done, he wouldn't be able to sell the horse. It would only be worth knacker price.

''Orl right then. You better do it,' was his surly reply.

When I got back to the surgery, I phoned through to the old practice, spoke to Mike and asked if I could borrow their tooth shears. I picked them up after my evening surgery hours, which nobody had taken advantage of.

Both Bill and Mike welcomed me and offered me a drink. They were sympathetic about the poor start I'd made. They tried to cheer me up by telling me it could go on like that for months, before it started to pick up. Once it did, it would snowball and I'd then be worried about having too much work.

The following morning after surgery, I loaded the tooth instruments into the car, drove over to the dealer's yard and once more negotiated the obstacle course to the line of stables.

It was a quiet old horse and it was not necessary to give it a tranquillising injection. I fitted a gag, a simple coil of metal, between the molars on the unaffected side of the mouth. This type of gag was usually well tolerated. The more expensive and complicated hinged type which acted against the incisor teeth was more fussy to fit. It also had a lot more projecting metal, which could be painful to the operator, if the horse swung its head about.

I laid the massive shears along the line of the molars, so that they took some of the weight, which was in the region of fifteen pounds. Even with the leverage afforded by the two foot long handles, I would not have had the strength to cut through the tooth. There was a closing device which fitted over the ends of the handles. It consisted of a large screw, turned by a tommy-bar.

Checking that the cutting end of the shears was in the right position, I started to tighten the screw. Four or five turns took up the slack, then the cutting edges started to bite. Another three turns and there was a whip-lash crack. The offending part of the tooth split off and fell out of the horse's mouth. The shears also fell out. I laid them on one side, picked up the piece of tooth and handed it to the dealer. He took it and examined it with distaste.

'There wasn't much to that then,' he commented.

'Not really,' I answered. 'Just having the right tools and knowing how to use them. That'll be three guineas please.'

'I still think it's a bit steep,' he grumbled, fishing into his trouser pocket. He brought out a thick roll of dirty fivers, peeled one off and handed it to me reluctantly

I gave him two pounds back. He said he didn't have the three shillings in silver.

CHAPTER NINETEEN

WOODEN TONGUE

IT was mid-way through my third week and September was over when Mr North from Manor Farm called me.

'My stockman, Harry, has been talking about you. We've got a heifer. She's been losing condition these past few weeks and dribbling a lot. Can you come and have a look at her and see what you can do? He's worried about the calves too. He lost two last week and now another one this morning.'

'She's not going lame too?' I asked, thinking of Foot and Mouth disease.

'No. Just dribbling and thin. When can you come?'

'Who did you have to do your veterinary work before?' I asked.

'That big firm of vets from Norton. It's a fair way for them to come and they charge plenty for it. I thought I'd try you as you're handy. There's another thing,' he continued. 'They never seem to send the same chap twice. One of them comes to look at a sick cow; the next day someone else turns up. I've got to go through the whole business of explaining the symptoms again. More often than not, I have to tell him what injections it's had the day before and whether it's improved or not.'

'I must ring them up to let them know that you want to change. It's professional etiquette.'

'You can if you want to. When can you come out?'

'I'll come out straight after surgery, in about an hour and a half.'

I got through on the telephone to one of the eight partners at Norton. They didn't seem unduly upset about losing this client, so I asked them if he paid his bills. They said he was a bit slow but paid after a few reminders.

The narrow lane leading to the farm was overgrown and the

hedges were untended. When a farmer was losing interest or control of his farm, the first things to suffer were the hedges.

The farmyard looked derelict. No cows were milked there now. Clumps of grass pushed up through the cracks in the concrete of the collecting yard and the milking parlour doors were hanging off their hinges. Ancient cowpats lay around the yard; dried and leathery, they looked like deflated footballs, with fine grey whiskers of mould sprouting from their edges.

I could now understand why the Norton practice was not upset at losing this client. An efficient farm was a stimulus to a veterinary surgeon; inefficiency was depressing. The animals were often neglected and their suffering, brought on by this neglect, unnecessary. Treatment prescribed would seldom be carried out and one's efforts were often wasted.

Harry the stockman met me with a welcoming smile.

His face looked like a sunset on a cut cornfield. It was a reddish, golden brown with three days' growth of golden stubble. His eyes crinkled and made him look entirely different from the time when he first met me as a stranger in the Spotted Cow, with a reserved, dead-pan expression. His teeth, false, were arresting. When I talked with him, I had to watch them, not his eyes. They were like stark, white tombstones and there was a time lag between their movement and the movement of his mouth, like a badly dubbed film.

'I managed to get 'im to call you to see the calves. 'E wants you to look at an 'eifer too. Shall we do 'er first?'

The heifer had not been brought in ready for me to examine. She was still running out at pasture with the rest of the bunch. We were going to waste a lot of time, bringing the whole bunch into the yard and isolating and penning up the one to be looked at.

Harry apologised for not having the heifer in and ready.

'The 'ole bugger only told me you was coming five minutes ago.'

We walked out to the field in which the heifers were grazing.

It was a still autumn morning. The pleasure of this backward rural setting made me forget my irritation at the delay and inefficiency.

We put up a covey of partridges. They streaked off flying low on blurred wings to plane down, out of sight and gunshot, on the far side of a boundary hedge. A heron lumbered across the sky, its trailing, skinny shanks, looking as though it had forgotten to retract its undercarriage.

The heifers, flicking their ears against the late-hatched flies, eyed us with suspicion. Two humans, one of them a stranger, boded ill. Their warm, bovine tranquillity was about to be disturbed.

Harry cooed lovingly to them, and they were partially reassured by this familiar voice. He turned and walked back towards the gate, calling gently to them. They followed him, while I circled round behind them and passively carried out a supporting role. The manoeuvre was carried out with no noise, shouting or fuss. It was not fear which drove them from their field, but their inquisitive nature which led them.

Once in the yard, Harry guarded the gate and they were allowed to escape back into the field in twos and threes, until there remained the one affected heifer, drooling saliva from her chin, and one companion for her, lest she panic on her own.

These two were driven into a loose-box and the affected heifer roped. When she was secure, her companion was allowed to return to the field.

Harry brought me a bucket of cold water, while I fetched the 'bulldogs', gag and a torch from the car. I handed him the 'bulldogs' to clamp into the heifer's nostrils. As I walked up past her flank, carrying the torch and gag, she let go a vicious, sweeping cow-kick, in spite of having her attention diverted by the 'bulldogs' in her nose. Her hard cloven hoof connected with a short, sharp crack against the side of my thigh boot, but it was the tail end of the kick and carried little weight.

I slid my hand into her mouth, grasped her tongue, pulled it towards me and twisted the tip upwards, so that it pressed against the roof of her mouth. This induced her to open her mouth wider and enabled me to peer inside.

Without the aid of the torch, I was able to see a roughened, ulcerated area on the upper surface of her tongue. I explored this ulcerated area with the finger tips of my other hand. It was hard and the surrounding tissue, which looked normal, was also hardened. I pulled my hand out, rasping my knuckles on the sharp edges of her molar teeth.

'She's got Wooden Tongue,' I said to Harry.

'I thought she 'ad. I told 'im so, two weeks ago. 'E said leave 'er, she may pick up. She's gorn down. Fast. If 'e'd 'ad 'er treated then, she'd be orl right now. As it is, it'll cost him a lot more to get 'er back into condition. What shall we do about it?'

'I'll give her an injection of sodium iodide. She'll need three altogether, at ten day intervals.'

' 'E won't like that. We 'ad one like this two years ago. The vet gave 'er a 'jection and she came up in a bloody great abscess on 'er neck. Something crool. She couldn't get 'er head down to feed and 'er front legs swelled up like tree trunks. We nearly 'ad to send 'er to the knacker.'

'That must have been because he missed the vein. If some of the sodium iodide gets under the skin, you do get a bloody great abscess.'

'Can't you give 'er these antibiotics?'

'No. Wooden Tongue's a fungus infection and it doesn't respond to antibiotics.'

' 'Ow do they get this fungus then?'

'It gets in through a break in the skin. It might be a thorn or a barley awn that does the initial damage.'

'Are you going to inject 'er now?'

'I haven't got the stuff with me. I can make it up when I get back to the surgery and we can give it to her tomorrow. I should leave her in here tonight. It'll save us having to catch her again. We'll have a look at the calves now. Where are they?'

'In the yard by the old bull-pen. They've been out in the Orchard meadow until last week. They were doing fine when we first turned 'em out, until about a month ago. Then they started to go back. We lost two last week, so 'e 'ad 'em brought into the yard. There was another one dead this morning. I'm

151

not surprised; it looked pretty sick yesterday morning. I told 'em about it, but 'e said leave 'im to see 'ow 'e gets on. 'E's seen how 'e's got on now orl right. The poor little bugger's dead. Like I said the other night; 'e's too mean to call you in until it's too late.'

'Before I post-mortem him, we'll have a look at the survivors.'

We stood and looked at them for a while over the yard gate. They were a poor looking bunch; ribby, tucked up and snotty-nosed. We climbed into the yard and walked over to them. As they moved away from us, several started coughing.

'Have they been doing much coughing?' I asked.

'Yes, a lot. They started a week or so after we turned 'em out.'

'We'll have a look at the dead one now. Can you get me a bucket of water?'

While he was getting the water, I collected soap, disinfectant and the post-mortem bag from my car.

The calf had been pulled out of the yard and lay against the wall in the tractor shed. It was a forlorn, pathetic bundle with glazed and sunken eyes. It had died unhappily and uncared for.

I took a large butcher's boning knife and steel out of the bag, flicked the edge up and down the steel a few times and laid it ready on top of the bag. Taking hold of the calf's death-stiffened legs, I rolled it on to its back, prised the legs apart and propped one of them against a straw bale. I then made a slashing cut through skin and muscle from the base of the neck, along the breastbone and abdomen to the pelvic brim. I cut a little deeper until the abdomen gaped open. Laying the knife on one side, I stuck my hand down through the incision and picked up a handful of intestines. They were still slightly warm. I pulled them out and had a look. They were not inflamed and appeared to be normal, so I pushed them back inside. Taking the knife again, I cut through the soft, cartilaginous bone along the side of the breast bone, forced the two sides apart and peered inside.

In the dim light, the lungs had dark red, almost black

152

patches on them. I cut through the wind-pipe and a few large blood vessels, pulled both lungs and heart out into the open and laid them on an empty plastic fertiliser bag which happened to be handy.

Harry had been standing watching me. His kindly reddened, weatherbeaten face showed no emotion, even though he had reared the calf and would have been able to pick it out of a bunch of twenty. He had seen death too often to be moved by it.

'This calf died of pneumonia,' I told him. 'Look at that lung, it's almost solid. Looks more like a bit of liver.'

I cut off a small piece and dropped it in the bucket of water. It sank.

'If it had been just congestion, caused by lying on one side after it died, that bit would have floated, even though it looked dark.'

I cut a bit off the other lung to demonstrate. I then used a pair of blunt-ended scissors to open up the windpipe. The lower end of it, where it branched off to each lung, was packed with greyish-white worms curled and knotted into bunches. I hooked several of them out on the end of the scissors and held them up in front of him.

'There's the cause of the trouble. Husk or parasitic bronchitis, caused by these worms, which developed into pneumonia.'

Harry looked at them, blinked once, but remained silent.

'The rest of the bunch are bound to be infected. If we don't treat them all and treat them soon, this won't be the last one to die. Those that don't die won't be much good.'

' 'Ow did those worms get there then?' Harry asked. ' 'Ow did they get in 'is tubes?'

'You must have had one or two cows or older stock grazing on that pasture during the summer. They will have had a few worms, living in their lungs; not enough to worry them or make them ill. These worms lay thousands of eggs a day; the cow coughs them up, swallows them and they pass out the other end with her droppings. They hatch out into larvae which crawl up the grass, especially when it's wet with dew. These calves have eaten the grass together with the larvae.'

153

'If they eat 'em they go into the stomach, don't they?' queried Harry, eyeing me suspiciously. 'Those worms were in 'is lungs.'

'They go into the stomach at first. Then the little sods burrow through the wall of the intestine, get into the bloodstream, and are carried round to the lungs.'

I put a bunch of the worms into an empty cigarette packet and took them up to the farmhouse.

Mr North was sitting in front of a roll-top desk which was submerged in bills and other bits of paper. He looked at the sample of worms with distaste.

'Is that what you found then?'

'Yes. Husk worms. The whole lot will need treating or you'll lose a lot more. Keep them yarded and give them an extra bit of grub. I wouldn't put any more calves on that pasture until it's been well rested. Take a hay crop off it next summer and then only use it for calves.'

'I don't think I'll have them treated. I'll take them all to market next Wednesday. Let someone else have the trouble.'

'Who's going to buy a bunch of calves like that? They look pretty rough now. By the time they've been shaken up in a cattle truck and driven around the market, they'll look a lot worse. Would you buy a bunch of calves that were coughing their heads off?'

'Perhaps you're right. You'd better treat them. What about the heifer? Harry thought it was Wooden Tongue?'

'Harry was right. He also said that you'd had some trouble with one two years ago. That was unfortunate, but if the injection is given properly into the vein, you'll find it'll be all right.'

He managed to produce a sour smile. 'If it isn't, I'll sue you.' I think he meant it.

CHAPTER TWENTY

THE EUTHANASIA BOX

ONE morning, a few days later and towards the end of surgery, the inspector of the local branch of an Animal Welfare Society walked into the waiting-room. The police-like authority of his smart, dark blue uniform was slightly undermined by a dirty pair of shoes.

'The Committee have asked me to get in touch with you,' he announced. 'They hope that you will be able to co-operate with them.' He had a pleasant friendly manner.

'If I can help them, I will,' I said. 'Tell me how.'

'They'd like to meet you first. There's a committee meeting tomorrow evening, seven o'clock at the Rural District Council offices. They would like you to attend and discuss things with them.'

There were eight of them, three men and five women seated at a long table when I was ushered in by the inspector.

I was introduced and invited to take a seat. The chairman, Major Pook-Green, was a fussy little grey-haired man with a well-trimmed moustache and a slight tic in the muscles of his right cheek. He was a retired business man, but had served in an Army Service Corps base camp during the first war, and insisted on being addressed as Major. Of the remaining members the five ladies seemed to be more interested in the social standing gained by being on the committee—animal welfare came a poor second. The other two men were a draper and a chemist.

Major Pook-Green declared the meeting open. The Hon. Secretary, Mrs Ethel Carp read the minutes of the last meeting. The Chairman then addressed me formally.

'I would like to put on record how pleased we are to have you here tonight. We have, in the past, had to rely on a distant and—ahem—not always reliable veterinary service. It gives us great pleasure to welcome you to our midst. Mrs Carp, perhaps you would like to put our first proposition to Captain Farrier.'

Mrs Carp rose from her chair.

'As you all know, we are too small a community to support an Animal Clinic. Now, thanks to Captain Farrier here, it looks as though our luck has changed. I propose that two evenings a week—we'll leave the actual days to Captain Farrier—he runs a free clinic on behalf of the society, at his surgery.'

This looked dangerous to me, but I remained silent for a while. I needed work. I needed publicity. I also needed money.

Mrs Carp did not remain silent.

'I'm sure Captain Farrier would willingly devote some of his valuable time to such a good cause.' She looked across the table at me and everyone else waited.

I stood up and addressed the Chairman.

'I'll be only too pleased to help you. And I'm prepared to charge you a reduced consultation fee and drugs at cost price, for those who genuinely cannot afford to pay.'

The room became suddenly very quiet. Even the whispering stopped.

'As it's for such a good cause, we thought you would do it for nothing,' said Mrs Carp with a tinge of aggression in her voice.

I had been expecting this and had prepared my defence.

'Before the days of the National Health Service,' I said, 'there were, throughout the country, various "Free" hospitals. They were free to those patients who felt they could not afford to pay for medical or surgical attention. They were supported financially by donations, flag days and perhaps the rates. The word "Free" applied only to the patients; the staff, doctors, surgeons, nurses, were paid normal fees. As there is no National Health Service for animals, I feel that your Society should operate on the same lines as the "Free" hospitals. You collect money on Flag Days, numerous wealthy patrons support you and leave you money in their wills. This money, or part of it, can be used to provide qualified help to animals whose owners are unable or unwilling to pay. No self respecting veterinary surgeon would deny treatment to a sick animal because its owner had no money. But some owners who are genuinely hard up, yet devoted to their animals, are too proud or too shy to go to a private veterinary surgeon and tell him, before or after the treatment, that they can't afford to pay him. This is where your society can do so much good. I am not wealthy, but if somebody can't afford to pay, I cannot turn him away. You can afford to pay and I shall charge you.'

Mrs Carp got her oar in first, before the Chairman had managed two twitches and a cough.

'We haven't very much money, you know. Most of it is taken up by administration. We did hope that you'd help us out without charging us.'

'Perhaps if you devoted less money to the administration there might be a little left over for the welfare of the animals.'

'We do try you know,' Mrs Carp gushed on. 'We organise a Charity Ball each year. It's one of the leading events of the year here. All the best people go. After all the expenses were taken out, we made nearly a hundred pounds last year. Most of that went on a new typewriter and a filing cabinet. I really feel that you should help us you know.'

'I will help you,' I said. 'You say that you are interested in the welfare of animals—so am I. If somebody comes to me with a sick animal and he can't pay me, I'll treat it for nothing. That will ease the burden on your society. I will work for you too, not for free but for a reduced charge. If you're hard up, why not sell the new typewriter?'

The Chairman stood up and endeavoured to wrest control of the meeting from Mrs Carp.

'I think we should go on to the next item on the agenda. The new euthanasia box for cats that Lady Flowater so kindly donated last month. I propose that we record our thanks to her. We are now able to put stray cats to sleep, humanely and painlessly.' He looked hopefully across at me.

'I'm sure Captain Farrier would help us operate this box if the Society supplied him with the chloroform.'

This was most unfortunate. I had already antagonised them

over the money angle, and this was going to be worse. But I had strong views on the subject of the so-called humane destruction of animals. Once more I addressed the chairman.

'Have you ever been shut in a cupboard or trapped in a lift? Do you suffer from claustrophobia? Think of the poor cat.'

Two of the lady members affected a sharp and audible intake of breath. 'It's a potentially wild animal,' I continued. 'It's an independent, freedom loving animal. It's usually unhappy or ill at ease with strangers. It's been incarcerated in a basket and brought to my surgery. It's away from its familiar environment and has been subjected to the frightening noise of the car or van in which it was transported. This cat may be unloved and unwanted. It may be a bastard, but it's still, as far as I'm concerned, an animal. I will talk to it. I will try to reassure it and make its last moments on this earth more tolerable. I will kill it but I shall be holding its paw and looking in its eyes. The slight prick of the needle necessary for the injection of an overdose of intravenous anaesthetic will barely be noticed. It will die easily.

'You propose that I should stuff it into a small airtight box and let it virtually choke to death on sickly-smelling chloroform.

'You call it humane, painless destruction because *you* can't see or hear it suffering, there's no blood, no mess—it's already emptied its bowels in fright on its journey to the box. You can't hear its hollow moans of terror or its frantic scrabbling at the sides of its lethal chamber before it dies.

'You're wrong. An animal can tolerate pain well; far more than a human, but it is highly sensitive to fear and suffers accordingly. I have attended cats which have been caught in a hay-cutter. All four legs have been chopped clean off. It's a black or tabby cylinder with four bloody stumps. If it had been a human, it would have been dead from shock or fright or both. The cat can't reason in those circumstances. It doesn't look at its terrible injuries with horror. It can't look ahead and visualise a life as a helpless cripple. I have stroked these cats, and there have been more than one, on the head and spoken to them. They have been reassured and they will purr. A cat in

158

agony or mental anguish will not purr. To be shut up alone in a tight box, would stop their purring.'

Two of the committee ladies left their places and made their erratic ways to the door; explaining over their shoulders that they had further appointments.

Ethel Carp stood up uncertainly.

'I don't know what we're going to say to Lady Flowater. She'll be frightfully upset if we don't make use of her very kind offer.'

I was by now at full gallop on my hobby-horse.

'Why not ask her to inaugurate it, by killing the first cat herself? She can put the poor sod in the box—her box—slam the lid down, pour in the chloroform and watch the box heave and jump as the cat, breaking its claws to the quick, tries to escape.'

The Chairman stood up and declared the meeting closed.

CHAPTER TWENTY-ONE

ANIMAL SUFFERING

A COLD wind blew across the market. It came from the east with a clear, pale blue sky. There was going to be frosty weather. The frost would break up the newly ploughed land and make a better seed-bed for the farmers' winter sown corn.

Bob Ferguson, now a firm and useful friend, since his dog made an uneventful recovery from its operation, huddled into his sheepskin jacket with his back to the wind.

'I can't think why you don't wear an overcoat or windcheater in this weather,' he said to me. 'It's enough to freeze the balls off a brass monkey. Why don't you?'

'I used to,' I told him. 'And I used to get one cold after another. Now I hardly ever get one. In freezing weather, I'd have to get out of a heated car at some farm, then take off my overcoat, jacket and sometimes my shirt and put on a cold, wet rubber apron. Now I only have to take off my jacket, the contrast isn't so great and I'm a little bit hardier.'

I noticed that the Inspector of the Animal Welfare Society was hovering in the background. He'd cleaned his shoes but was spoiling his handiwork by rubbing the sole of one across the instep of the other. He caught my eye and offered me a bleak smile. I smiled back at him. He came over and joined us; a little diffidently, I thought. I introduced him to Bob.

'I'll go and flog some more tractors and leave you two to talk shop,' said Bob after a few minutes.

There was an awkward silence, while we both gazed into the middle distance. I'd noticed that he wore on his uniform the Africa Star with a shiny 8 on it and the Italian Campaign medal. To break the ice, I asked him which mob he was with.

'Wiltshire Yeomanry,' he answered. 'We went out to Palestine with our horses in '39. Then we were mechanised.'

'It's a small world, isn't it?' I answered. 'I had some of your horses to look after, when you had to give them up. I also had to look at your Regimental mascot once.'

Inspector Alan Brown laughed; the ice was well and truly broken.

'He was a very discerning goat. He'd eat any cigarette except the Free Issue "V's". Offer him one of those; even if you tried to fool him by taking it out of a "Lucky Strike" packet, he'd take one bite and spit it out. You were RAVC were you, Sir?'

'I was and you don't have to call me "Sir". I'm plain "Mister" now.'

He chuckled and I knew he was on my side.

'You certainly put the cat among the pigeons at the meeting the other night. They called an emergency meeting on the following night to discuss you.'

'My little outburst might have done some good then; it may have made a slight crack in their tight, complacent little shells?'

'I don't think it's done you much good,' he laughed. 'Mrs Carp thinks you're a "horrid, rude man". She wanted to get the committee to report you and your bad behaviour to the College of Veterinary Surgeons. She hates you almost as much as she hates that other Animal Welfare Society which send their treatment van to the market here each week.'

'She can hate me if she likes. I can almost take it as a compliment. But why should she hate the other Welfare Society?'

'She hates them because people give them money. She thinks her Society ought to have it all. She resents them for having muscled in on the act.'

'Perhaps I was a little tactless the other night, but I'm afraid I cannot tolerate fools, and anyway tact is not part of my job. So many of your members are misguided benighted fools. They're relatively harmless and by accident they do some good. They could do so much more good, but they're running in blinkers. Firstly most of them only join because of the social kudos. Secondly, as I pointed out, perhaps a little vehemently, the other night, they can't or won't see that animals suffer far more mentally, from fear or anguish, than they do physically. Because they can't see them suffering, they think everything is all right. Thirdly, they try and credit animals with the same reasoning power as "homo sapiens". They see a lot of hens in battery cages and think it's cruel. Hens are cruel. As cruel or even more so than humans. Under farmyard conditions or free range, they bully each other. There is an established "pecking order" and the weaker members, at the bottom of the list, suffer horribly. In battery cages, hens are protected from their neighbours. A happy hen lays more eggs. Your society makes a lot of noise about battery hens. I think that they resent the fact that it is commercially successful. Perhaps they consider that the poor hens are being exploited. The reason it is successful is because the standard of hygiene is higher, there is less disease and the hens are contented. The hen has a tiny brain. It is concerned only with its hour to hour, day to day existence. It is fed, watered and protected. It is in a socialist utopia. Many of your society and other emotional bird-brains maintain that a battery cage is a prison cell with a life sentence in solitary for its occupant. The hen can only appreciate it as a sanctuary. Would you advise the general public, and poultry farmers in particular to organise and support cock-fighting?

'In a cock-fight the contestants are more or less equal. They do not suffer fear. They're aggressive little bastards; intent on destroying each other, to gain supremacy. They are willing to die in the attempt.

'Yet you campaign to persuade these same poultry farmers to release their birds from the security of a battery cage and expose them to the vicious dominance of their fellows; to a short painful life of pecking, misery and death.

'Once again, you do not see the bullying and cruelty that occurs between poultry on free range. It occurs perhaps in the far corner of the field—like schoolboys fighting behind the cricket pavilion. Because you don't see it, you don't recognise it. Cock-fighting is a "spectator" sport. Though far less suffering occurs, it can be seen—therefore it must be condemned.

'Some of your fraternity object to the Grand National. "It's

162

cruel" they say, because you can see a horse take a tumble and break a leg. The horse does not have the mental ability to visualise the dangers that lie ahead and luckily, some of the jockeys are similarly equipped. Those that do, are very brave men. If a horse unseats its jockey, does it stop, breathe a sigh of relief and pack it in? No. It continues round the course of its own free will.'

We sat at the bar in the Cattle Market Inn, elbow to elbow, ruminating over our pints of bitter.

Hanging over the fly-speckled, gilt-edged mirror at the back of the bar, was a corn-dolly. It was stained brown from its long exposure to the smoky atmosphere. The wheat ears hanging below it, had lost most of their grain and looked limp and bedraggled. When new, it would have been a shining, pale gold ornament with the full ears of wheat bristling beneath it. It may once have stood atop a corn rick. But it was larger than usual and more elaborate, so it had probably been made to decorate a church or barn at Harvest Festival.

With the advent of the combine harvester and grain driers, corn ricks, either round or rectangular, were a rare sight on farms. The cost of labour and the increased tempo of farm life made it uneconomical to build them. In any event, there were now very few farm labourers with the ability to build a rick, let alone thatch it and fashion a corn-dolly to add the finishing touch to their skilled handiwork.

We had had two good rick builders on the farm in Devon and they used to vie with each other to make the neatest ricks. At the end of harvest, they would spend many hours making large corn-dollies. They'd chosen the longest, unbent straws from the standing wheat and kept them carefully until harvest was over. I remembered watching their gnarled and horny hands with heavy square fingers ending in blackened, broken finger-nails, bending and weaving the six delicate straws into intricate, symmetrical patterns. They had tried to teach me, but mine always ended up dented or lop-sided.

It looked so easy when they did it and the end product was immaculate. The curving, convex spirals with the fine sharp edges fashioned out of fragile straw were a testimonial to their innate sensitivity. This, because of their shyness, was seldom seen in everyday life.

In my uncle's absence they tried to teach me to build a corn-rick. I was quite proud of my first effort. I organised the brushwood, left over from hedge-trimming, into a tangled circle—it was to be a round rick—to make the base. This would stop the bottom sheaves from rotting on the damp earth. This was covered with some old straw, left over from last year's harvest.

The high-loaded wagon with a gleeful, grinning, farmboy perched on top of the swaying load stopped alongside my humble base. With the carter and the boy both pitching, the dry sheaves rattled down on me. I had to keep the middle up so that the outside line of sheaves had their butts sloping down to stop driving rain from seeping into the rick and ruining the corn. If I kept it too high, they slipped off and I was cursed heartily, yet in jest, for giving them the trouble of pitchforking them up again. At six feet high and in between wagon loads, I slid off my embryo rick to survey my handiwork; I thought it looked pretty good. One or two sheaf butts were protruding more than they should. With a plank of wood I bashed them back into line. It was coming out nicely from the base, though it was not precisely a circle. It looked more like a distorted tear-drop. It was too late to change it now, but I thought I'd do better with the roof.

Another four feet and I could start to roof in. I was now getting higher than the wagon and the pressure was easing off. They had to pitch the sheaves up to me now and they weren't coming so fast. Topping it off was the worst part. Only one sheaf at a time came up but I was standing on a slippery, angled surface, fourteen feet above the ground. Two more sheaves filled in the foot-hold my weight had made halfway up the roof. Apart from thatching and the corn-dolly, it was a complete rick.

I slid carefully down the slope of the roof until my feet projected over the eaves and made contact with the high wooden lade at the end of the wagon. I climbed down the rungs of the lade, on to the wagon floor and vaulted on to the

ground. I was well pleased with myself. I stood back and surveyed my first-born rick with pride. Matthew, under whose
supervision, I had worked, was kind to me and said it wasn't
too bad for a beginner. My uncle saw it and, not knowing its
architect, accused Matthew of having drunk too much cider.

That night I had a bad dream. I woke up in a cold sweat.
My beloved rick had fallen over. It seemed so real and vivid, I
had to get up and see. I must have looked a ridiculous sight, in
a dressing gown with skinny white ankles protruding out of my
heavy farm boots as I tried to tip-toe out of the house. Sport
grumbled at me as I shuffled past him and some damn fool
young cockerel thought it was morning and started to crow. I
got to my rick and there it was, in the moonlight, standing
proudly—a beautiful sight. Happily I returned to bed.

It was another three days before it started to slip. As the
sheaves settled down it began to tilt sideways. I pretended not
to notice it—I refused to believe it. Matthew was more practical. He wedged two strong poles against it, to stop any further
movement and its complete collapse. With this support, it
stopped its slide and held up until threshing time, but it spoilt
my autumn. I had to pass it many times and it was a source of
shame.

The professional thatcher, who did not concern himself with
corn ricks, but thatched farm and other houses, with straw or
Norfolk reed depending on the financial status of the owner,
had a dog. He was a terrier of sorts called Spot. He was
mainly white, with a black patch over and including one eye
and another over his back which looked like a saddle which
had slipped.

He lived in the village but his master did not confine him to
the house. His hobby was killing rats; he was a dedicated rat
catcher. He would always follow the threshing tackle, knowing
full-well that where it stopped, corn-ricks would be opened up
and the rats they harboured would have to flee.

When the threshing tackle was idle, he would tag along with
his master. He would sit around all day, doing nothing, share a
little of his lunch-time cheese and then follow him home in the
evening. Apart from trotting along behind the pony and trap,

he had a lazy time.

When the threshing tackle was on the move he forsook his master. He became a changed character, a ball of fire. Every rat that scurried from the rick was doomed. There would be a blur of white as he sped after it. A quick chop and a shake and he would stalk confidently back to wait for the next one. As the rick got down to the last few layers of sheaves, the remaining rats, who had not had the courage to desert their sinking ship before, were forced to leave. At this stage, he did not return to the rick, but circled warily around it, so that he could see from a distance if more than one rat broke cover at the same time. He would rush in and intercept one and still have time to catch the second before it gained cover. When the last rat had left the rick, and not before, he would trot happily home.

We had four ricks to thresh, including my lop-sided one, which for no good reason was left until last. Spot had notched up twenty rats from the first three ricks and sat waiting expectantly as the thatch was stripped off the last one. A rat was sheltering under the thatch. It scurried between the knees of the thresher's mate, flopped heavily on to the ground and travelled no more than two yards before Spot pounced.

He shook it once, which was all that was necessary, dropped it, turned round and padded off home, before we had even started threshing. He had never done a thing like this before. He always stayed to the end and until the last rat was killed. We all stopped and looked at him.

Matthew, my master rick builder, commented, a little unkindly I thought, that he probably couldn't stand the sight of my badly-made tilting rick.

We continued to demolish it until the last sheaf had been fed into the whirling drum of the threshing machine. Not a single rat appeared. It was most unusual, but the only rat in the whole rick had been the one under the thatch. We all wondered why. Matthew, of course, commented that no self-respecting rat would consider living in a rick like that. They wouldn't feel safe in it. What intrigued us most was the fact that Spot had, as always, stayed until the last rat and no longer. How did he know?

My reverie, which started with the corn-dolly, had lasted through a whole pint of beer, I ordered two more. Alan, the Inspector of the Animal Welfare Society, was gazing somewhat vacantly into the gilt-edged mirror.

'You're very quiet,' I said.

Alan sipped his beer thoughtfully.

'Do you often have to call in a second opinion?' he asked.

'Not very often now. But if I am stumped, I don't hesitate to recommend it to the owner. It's nothing to be ashamed about, two minds are usually better than one and I find that most owners appreciate it if you're honest with them, if you put their animal's welfare before your own pride. You don't lose clients—that is clients worth having—by telling them you don't know, providing you make every effort to find out. You can lose them much more easily by being too casual and not giving their animal a thorough examination.

'There is a form of communication between patient and vet, once he has gained some experience. It is the silent language of the sick animal. It may be a form of extra-sensory perception or perhaps it is based on subconscious reasoning. Jig-saw pieces of vaguely remembered past cases, seen as a student and later, in practice, snap into position. The picture is revealed with startling and unexpected clarity, when the patient is first observed and before the owner has spoken. It is seldom wrong.

'A talkative owner may blur or even disarrange this pattern. One who has already, in his own mind, diagnosed the trouble, will often insist on demonstrating his remarkable diagnostic skill. He usually does this before the veterinary surgeon of his choice has had a chance to speak. Whether he is right or wrong, it is usually possible to pick up the pieces he has scattered and reassemble them.

'It is then necessary to pretend that you don't know. To carry out a thorough examination. If this charade is not carried out, the owner will be dissatisfied. He will think that you are not being conscientious in your work. He may even consider you to be flippant, not worth your fee and he will tell all his friends so. The fact that you are right and that the treatment is successful, cuts no ice. You will be branded as being too casual and your success explained away as luck, not skill.

'There are other times, when the pieces do not make a picture. There may be gaps in it, or occasionally it may be totally incomprehensible. A thorough examination—very necessary this time—may reveal the missing pieces. Close questioning of the owner, sifting his evidence, may clarify the picture. If, after all this, the screen still remains blank, it is then the time to admit defeat and seek another opinion.'

Alan finished his beer, and suggested we have another, but it was getting late.

We left the bar and returned to the market.

'What are you doing for lunch?' Alan asked me.

'I'll go back to the surgery and cook myself some eggs and bacon,' I told him.

'Would you like to take pot-luck with us? It won't be very much, but you're welcome to what's going.'

I followed his van as he drove home and parked behind it in the narrow street. The house was small and old-fashioned, one of a long terrace, and the front door opened directly into the front parlour. It was clean, bright and had a happy atmosphere.

We fed in the kitchen. Lunch as he had said was simple but very good. Thick green-pea soup—home made. Instead of croutons, his wife had fried-up bits of bacon rind, until they were brittle, charred and almost black. They made an effective contrast to the smooth, thick soup. Apart from cheese, the soup was the only course, but there was more than enough of it and it was very satisfying.

'Has your Hon. Secretary been in touch with Lady Flowater, about the euthanasia box?' I asked him, while we were drinking our coffee.

Alan laughed. 'No. Apart from a formal letter, thanking her. I don't think they'll tell her what you said about it. I think they'll let the whole thing slide.'

'What's Lady Flowater like?' I asked him.

'She's a very nice person, but she seems to be a little bit absentminded. Give her a few weeks and she'll probably have forgotten that she's ever given us the box.'

'What does her husband do for a living?' I asked.

'Sir Oscar? He's a real country gentleman. Nice chap, bags of money. He's Master of the local pack of Foxhounds. They meet twice a week. He's also got two farms. He doesn't run them himself, he's got a manager for each one. He rears calves and barley beef on one. The other is mainly poultry, battery system.'

'That's interesting,' I remarked. 'The husband of the Hon. President of the local branch of your Society, not only hunts foxes but has battery hens. What does the "Most Noble" Mrs Ethel Carp your Hon. Secretary think about that?'

'You're not the first person to ask that,' said Alan sipping his coffee. 'My predecessor also queried it. He was a very conscientious man but perhaps he was a little aggressive or too honest, anyway it didn't do him much good; he got the sack.'

'Who sacked him?' I asked. 'And why?'

'The Committee,' said Alan. 'Because he told Mrs Carp, rather forcibly I understand, that Lady Flowater, having a husband who hunted and kept battery hens, should not be Hon. President. He reckoned that it would give the society a bad image. He threatened to report the matter to Head Office. Silly of him—Head Office obviously knew about it and chose to ignore it.'

'If Mrs Carp is so interested in Animal Welfare, that she devotes so much of her time to being Hon. Secretary, I should have thought she would have supported the Inspector,' I said.

'You would, wouldn't you. But she didn't. Lady Flowater occasionally invites her to tea. She recognises and talks to her when the meet in town. Mrs Carp sits near her and Sir Oscar at the head table at the Annual Ball. All this is vitally important to her social standing and her neighbours are most impressed. All this would be lost if the Committee, however politely, asked Her Ladyship to resign. Major Pook-Green, the Chairman, felt the same, so they persuaded the other members to rally round and poor old Inspector Jones was out on his neck.'

'What are your views on battery hens and foxhunting?' I

asked him.

'I'm employed by the Society, so it's better for me if I don't have any opinions on anything. Strictly between ourselves, I agree with you; I can't see anything wrong with battery hens. As for fox hunting, I used to be a hunt servant before the war. That's why I joined up with the Wiltshire Yeomanry.'

'As an old hunt servant and now as an Inspector of an Animal Welfare Society, your views on fox hunting should be worth hearing,' I prompted. 'Are you for or against?'

'It depends how you look at it,' said Alan. 'It can't be much fun for the fox, when he gets caught, which is seldom. As a means of killing foxes, it's uneconomical and inefficient. Shooting, trapping or poisoning are more efficient ways. Though the fox suffers far more from poisoning or trapping and from shooting, unless he's killed outright, the public don't see it happening, so they don't think it's cruel and don't make any fuss about it. From the point of view of offending public opinion, these ways are better. A pack of foxhounds in full cry attracts attention. The hunt, or some of them, are seen to be enjoying themselves. This, I think, is what antagonises a certain type of person and they are the ones who make a lot of noise about it. If I was a fox, and was given the choice, I'd far rather be hunted than poisoned, trapped or even shot, unless he was a very good marksman behind the gun. Being hunted, I'd have a good chance of survival if I used my wits and a fox is foxy. If he is caught, the end, though very unpleasant, is quick. Anyway, why should you feel pity for him, if he's pulled to pieces by a pack of hounds in a matter of seconds. He's a bloodthirsty little bastard himself.

'Carnivorous animals normally only kill for food, and only when it's necessary. Humans kill and keep on killing for pleasure—it's called sport. Foxes also kill for sport. Look what happens when a fox gets into a chicken house. No doubt he's hungry but he doesn't just kill one hen and take it home to eat it. He kills the lot. Rips 'em to pieces—feathers and blood everywhere.'

'If they're in battery cages he doesn't,' I said. 'He wouldn't get through the wire.'

'What are your views on hunting?' Alan asked.

'The same as yours with regard to foxes. But I strongly disapprove of deer, otter hunting and digging badgers.'

'They also do a lot of damage. Why differentiate?'

'Deer can damage crops and plantations, but they're gentle, timid creatures; not bloodthirsty and cunning. If it's necessary to keep their numbers down, it can be done more effectively and humanely by shooting. They make a bigger and better target than a fox.'

'What about otters?'

'I'm not so sure about otters. They're delightful animals and it would be a tragedy to eliminate them. But if I was a fisherman, I might view them in a different light, if a pair of them happened to visit my stretch of water. The sight of fifteen or twenty good fish, glinting in the grass on the river bank with just one bite out of each of them is a horrible sight to a keen fisherman. If they caught and ate one or two, it wouldn't seem quite so bad. But there are times when they behave like a fox and kill wantonly, for pleasure.

'Not being a fisherman, I can find some excuse for them. A fox is a solitary, dedicated, calculating killer. I don't think an otter is. On his own he will kill a fish to eat and leave it at that. The trouble begins when there are two of them. Like two small boys, they egg each other on; daring each other to commit further acts of mischief. A pair of dogs can be the same. It's only rarely that a single dog will turn into a sheep killer. But a pair who have teamed up and trotted off looking for adventure can be lethal to sheep, even though individually they are well behaved and the apple of their owner's eye.

'I think otters are the same and I think it is wrong to condemn them for a brief lapse in their normal good behaviour.'

CHAPTER TWENTY-TWO

THE FOX

ONE night I dreamed I was a fox. I was young and handsome with a fine brush, light, agile walk and my first winter's coat was a thick, red-brown.

I had left home some weeks ago but the memories were still fresh. My mother was a very good-looking vixen; she was also clever. Before we were born, she had made her earth under the tangled roots of a large old beech tree. The inside was snug and dry and the entrance very narrow. It was to save all our lives.

It was a late September morning. Mother had been back home since dawn, several hours ago. She'd brought back a good sized rabbit. We had finished eating and my sister, brother and myself were having a good old game with the skin; growling and tugging at it. My brother tended to be a bit rough when he played—his teeth were like needles.

Mother was lying watching us in the dim light which filtered down the hole. We felt her stiffen and saw the hairs rise along the back of her neck and down her spine. We stopped playing and looked at her inquisitively. She took no notice of us but crept nearer to the hole so that most of the light was blocked out. I remember vividly, seeing, in the almost total dark, the faint outside light shining on her large canine tooth as she curled up her lip. We began to be frightened by her change of smell and attitude. We huddled together behind her, wide-eyed and hardly daring to breathe.

A most unusual and unpleasant scent came in from the outside—Mother told us afterwards that it was the smell of man and warned us always to avoid it, but we knew it meant danger before she told us.

Muffled sounds and scuffling noises had been coming into

172

our earth for several minutes. Mother stayed crouching at the entrance. She was completely silent—she was not even panting, though I'm sure she wanted to—we wanted to as well, but we sensed that we must follow her example.

The light, reflected off Mother's bared, snarling teeth went out and a deafening, high pitched yapping came down the hole and beat against our ears. For the first time, Mother growled; it was very low pitched and, to us, sounded very dangerous— she must have been very angry. She edged herself forward, up the hole as the scuffling noises grew louder. Now, no light at all came in. We didn't mind the dark—we were used to it, but the loud, hot, panting noises, the high pitched whimpers and the occasional yapping, excited barks, made us very frightened. We crouched in the far corner of the earth. I gave my sister a small, wet lick across her mask, to try and reassure her.

Suddenly Mother shot halfway up the hole. There were many sharp, snapping noises then a high pitched yelp. Some light came flooding in as Mother backed down the hole. She smelled of blood. She lay panting and watching for a while then turned herself round and gave us each a comforting nudge and a lick. We felt much happier and braver too. I went across, looked up the hole and gave a fierce bark, but it didn't come out right—it was too squeaky.

The sound of digging and scraping of soil sounded very loud. Mother moved back to guard the entrance. It went on for a long time, slowly getting closer. Then it stopped.

When Mother had first dug out this earth, she had made the entrance tunnel go between two thick roots of the tree, leaving just enough room for her to squeeze through. They couldn't dig any nearer to us.

Mother had been giving us each another lick, when the loud scuffling and panting started again. It sounded very close this time. She spun round with a really vicious growl, scattering us all over the bed. I got her hind foot in my stomach which knocked all the wind out of me. I know it was an accident but it could have been serious—I was now not able to help her fight to defend our home.

The close, hot, smelly breath of a dog filled the air. As I lay panting against the back wall, I could see the black and white muzzle and bared teeth of a hunt terrier. Mother was snapping and snarling at him. But she was quicker than he was. He yelped and continued to yelp as he retreated back up the hole. The smell of blood was strong now.

When more light came down the hole and it fell quiet outside I got up and went over to the entrance to have a sniff round. I was feeling better now and could help take over guard duties.

There was quite a big pool of blood right at the entrance, it was oozing down into the earth. Lying beside it was a piece of an ear with white hairs over most of it and a few black ones at the tip. Large spots of blood lay at intervals up the entrance passage. I gave a warning bark up the hole, to let them know I was there and ready for them. I then returned to Mother who lay panting on the floor. She had a nasty bite wound on her lip and several scratches on her mask. I licked them better before returning to take up guard.

Nothing happened for a long time. Then there was a loud thumping noise overhead. The earth shook and bits of dirt pattered down from the ceiling. It was very frightening and I returned to Mother to make sure she was all right. She didn't seem at all alarmed and just lay there, keeping one eye on the entrance. They were trying to dig down to us from the top, but we were well protected by the gnarled roots of the old beech tree and she knew we were safe. After a few hours they gave up and went home.

When I first left the earth, I was a little unsure of myself. I soon learned to exist—I had to. I travelled many miles, mainly at night. Having been reared in semi-darkness I felt more at home in the dark. I drank from ponds, rain-water puddles and streams but I was getting hungry.

Across a field I could see the outline against the night sky, of a farmhouse roof with its square, barren chimneys. I circled round it and a dog barked. I knew he couldn't be barking at me because I was down wind. I crouched low listening in the crisp autumn darkness. The stars were bright, close and

174

friendly. I heard the rustle of feathers nearby.

I lay quiet. Close to me was a wire netting enclosure with a wooden shed on one side of it. There was more rustling of feathers and a few anxious, low pitched clucks. I'd tasted chicken before—it was good. The feathers were irritating but the flesh was warm.

It took me only a few minutes to dig under the wire-netting of the run. A plank with convenient footholds led up to a small black hole in the side of the chicken-house. I waited and looked around me for a while—I didn't want to fall into a trap. All was quiet. The dog had stopped barking. I crept up the wooden ramp. The rustling of feathers became more agitated and the clucking noises assumed a different and more urgent pitch. I only wanted one—just enough to stave off the pangs of hunger. They didn't give me a chance. The whole house exploded into a mass of flying feathers and high pitched squawks. I felt that I had to keep them quiet or there would be trouble. It didn't take long but the mess—blood and feathers —was dreadful. The last one I killed, I took with me. I parked it by the hole under the wire netting, struggled under, turned round and pulled it through. It was a tidy weight, but I held my head high and let it drag between my forelegs. I carried it well over half a mile before I stopped to enjoy it.

I lived well through that winter, even though there were days when I had to exist on beetles and the odd mouse.

I had one brush with the hunt—excuse the dreadful pun, but even foxes have a sense of humour.

I caught the scent of them, before I heard them, and I heard them well before I saw them. The hounds were streaming out in front of the pink coated huntsmen, with the rest of the field close behind, moving at a nicely controlled hand-canter. The short brassy notes of the huntsman's horn were thrown back from the chalky walls of a quarry. I was down wind of them and they had another half-mile to go before the pack crossed and picked up my scent. They would then turn left-handed and be in full cry after me. I was feeling fresh and confident and I'd give them a fair run for their extortionate subscriptions. It was like playing with children, but I had an uneasy feeling

175

that, if I made a mistake, they would turn out to be nasty vicious little children—but I wasn't going to err and give them their full satisfaction.

I was two furlongs ahead and I heard the 'View Halloo' as they sighted me. I was going fast, running well over good going; with the sight they increased to a split-arsed gallop. But I knew the country as well as or better than they did. They were less than a furlong behind when I hit the well-used tarmac road. A lorry driver and his mate, high up in their cab, pointed at me and laughed in astonishment. Their lorry, belching diesel fumes and dripping oil, sped past me. I tucked in behind it and got hooted at by a following car. They could have run me down but they didn't. They swerved round me and slowed down to my pace. The bright excited faces of two children pressed their noses to the rear window as they watched me. Two furlongs up the road with its overpowering alien smells would have that pack of hounds well and truly foxed. I then turned off the road into the flood ditch at the side, doubled back and crept through a drainage culvert under the road to the other side. I sat and watched the whole pack in full cry, tearing through the barbed wire into the wood on the other side of the road. I was worried for a moment when a small girl on a pony who had lagged behind and lost her way, trotted past me. She looked me straight in the eyes and trotted on; I don't think she'd ever seen a fox before. She probably thought I was a Corgi.

Spring was exhilarating. Fox-hunting—not that it mattered —was nearly over. Rabbits, bewitched by sex, were less careful and one didn't have to dig down through the snow to find the odd beetle.

I caught up with a very interesting scent. I padded smartly on—ears akimbo—after it. She was beautiful—full brush, in spite of the hard winter, narrow, delicate, elegant mask. There was one snag. An old dog fox was paying court to her. He was several winters older than I was and, no doubt, very wily. I wasn't feeling very brave so I circled around them discreetly. She saw me, sat down and nonchalantly scratched her ear. I took my courage in both paws and advanced. Lover boy saw me. His hackles rose—just like Mother's when she was fighting off the hunt terrier—but he didn't approach me. I circled nearer and pee'd nonchalantly on his territory.

He took the insult as it was intended and stalked, stiff-legged, towards me. He was bigger than me and I had half-a-mind to skip off. Looking past him, I saw the vixen; she was looking at me with interest. I had no option; I had to fight.

Menacingly, he continued his slow stiff walk towards me. If he'd stayed still for a moment, it would have given me time to think, to work out a plan of attack. But he didn't. So I rushed at him, flinging myself at his throat. He side-stepped and got me behind the ear as I shot past. I felt his teeth slice through my skin and tear out again as he jerked my head to one side and I rolled over in a tangled heap of legs and brush. I was on my back when he rushed at me, but he mistimed his speed and distance. I got him firmly by the testicles as he slid over me. I hung on and gave them a savage crunch. He grunted heavily, arched his back and clamped his teeth firmly through the skin and muscle of my forearm. The pressure of his jaws was so great, I thought he'd break the bone. I spat out his hairy scrotum, twisted my head round and clamped my teeth on to his windpipe. I held on, tightened my grip and held on some more. Slowly, the pressure on my forearm slackened. My jaws were aching but I hung on. His tongue was going black and his saliva was dripping into my eye. When his mouth went slack I pulled my leg out. I held on until he collapsed on top of me. Shrugging him off, I limped over to our lone spectator. We went off together.

Her earth wasn't as good as Mother's but the attention I received was sublime. There was a two inch long gash in the skin behind my ear and deep puncture wounds in my foreleg. She licked and tended them until they healed.

She bore me four beautiful cubs. It was her second litter; she'd had two cubs the previous summer, but we didn't talk about those.

Ours were two weeks old and their eyes were open. They were golden-red bundles of fluff, tiny little pointed masks and big eyes. Their mother was always hungry. The rabbits in our area had been almost wiped out by Myxomatosis, poultry farmers were increasingly on the alert and food was short. Both of us were fully occupied hunting for food.

One evening, I left her suckling the cubs and went out on the prowl. Not far from our earth and lying across one of our well-used tracks was a dead rabbit. It did not have the bulging eyes and bloated look of one that had died of Myxomatosis. There was some blood on its ears. It looked to me as though it had been shot. If it had been shot in the head, it would not have run far. There were footprints and the smell of man near-by. I wondered why the person who had shot it had not picked it up. The way it was lying and its smell made me suspicious. I left it alone, circled round it and padded on into the woods. I found a pheasant's nest with a clutch of twelve eggs. I noted its position, took one egg and holding it very gently in my mouth, ran back to report my good fortune.

I met her as I came out of the wood. She was crouched by the side of the track, tearing the guts out of the dead rabbit. Feeding four lusty cubs was a big drain on her and she was famished. I think her hunger overcame her normally suspicious and careful nature. I dropped the egg and ran up to her. She continued feeding so I tried to nuzzle her away. She misunderstood me and thought I was trying to take it from her. She curled her lip—a thing she'd never done to me before—and gave me a warning growl. Picking up the remains, she ran away from me. She had gone about twenty paces, when she dropped it, stood still and tried to vomit. Her legs stiffened as a violent cramping pain spread from her stomach all over her body. She was fully conscious but incapable of co-ordinated movement as the griping, tetanic convulsions shook her whole body. All four legs were rigidly extended, her brush quivering and her head and neck arched backwards. The muscles of her chest were held tightly in spasm and she died of suffocation in a few minutes.

The cubs, our beautiful cubs, were not weaned and were too young to take anything but vixen's milk. I was bewildered. I couldn't return to the earth to watch them die slowly of starvation. I took off and spent the rest of the summer raiding chicken houses.

In November, I met up with my old rival again. The circumstances were very different from the time when we had fought over possession of the vixen.

He was being hunted and was hard pressed. He looked beaten; his tongue lolled out of his mouth, he was wet and bedraggled and his brush trailed in the mud.

He was working his way up the side of a stream. I was on the other side and he didn't see me. When he drew level, I gave a short bark. He stopped and looked at me. I moved back from the bank. He accepted my invitation and crossed over to my side. He was so exhausted that he had difficulty climbing the shallow bank out of the stream. Having crossed the water, his trailing scent would be interrupted. It would only gain him a brief respite as the hounds would soon pick it up again along the other bank.

I was feeling fresh and in good spirits. I crossed the stream at the same point as he had and continued his old trail along the bank—across a water-meadow, up through a spinney and out on to a small grass covered hill. I stopped and looked back to the stream below me. The hounds passed our changeover point without a check. They were now, although they didn't know it, after a fresh fox; I'd lead them a merry dance.

An hour and a half later, I was beginning to regret my noble gesture. Hounds were being hunted well and the huntsman was not being fooled by my attempts to throw them off the scent by crossing streams and using roads.

I was tiring and they were gaining on me. I was coming out on to open downland now and was not far from my birthplace. The thought of that safe and friendly earth, spurred me on. The sight of me streaking across the open country spurred them on too and they continued to gain on me. The sombre shadows of the beech wood enfolded me as I made straight for my old familiar home. I skidded up to the hole and was struck with horror: it had been well and truly stopped, with a tree-trunk, earth and stones. Panic welled up inside me; like my old rival, my tongue was lolling out and I was now bedraggled and exhausted. Hounds were close behind and ready for the kill. I crept out of the far side of the wood. The barbed wire perimeter fence delayed them and a deep ditch afforded me some cover. It led down, by the side of a rough cart track, to a village. Halfway down this ditch, I met my salvation. A sheep had got on to its back and had died. The carcase was decomposing and village dogs had been feeding from it. I rolled myself in the putrid mess, making sure my pads were well covered in slime.

I'd thought of running down to the village and hiding in a disused pigsty, or, better still a goat pen. Either of these would have camouflaged my scent. If I hadn't come across the dead sheep, I would have had no option. But this huntsman was no fool; he was hunting by instinct as well as scent. He was thinking ahead of me—as I'd already found out to my cost. I don't think he appreciated the value of the dead sheep. I reckoned that he expected me to go on to the village. So, at the next bend, I climbed out of the ditch and doubled back up the hill to the wood. My main worry was that I would meet the tail end of the field—the stragglers. But they would be the ones that hunted for snob value—to enhance their social standing—they wouldn't know a bloody fox from a rabbit. Two of them saw me. One of them pointed at me and they trotted primly on. I followed my old scent to the edge of the wood, scrambled into the cover and sat and looked back down the hill.

Hounds checked at the sheep. They cast around, then the Whipper-in took them on. They'd lost me, and they ran on to the village. I felt sorry for any stray cat they encountered.

I lay low for a couple of days, to get my strength back. Hunger then tempted me down to the village and the hen houses.

I knew my way around most of the gardens and back yards; I knew the ones who had dogs and which dogs were free and which chained.

This time I chose a small-holding on the outskirts of the village. I'd raided it three or four months ago and they should have had time to restock the chicken run. I lay watching and listening outside the wire. There was no sound apart from the rustling of feathers. There was a weak spot in the wire-netting

—I remembered it from the last time. I eased myself under it and took one step towards the ramp leading up to the hole in the chicken house.

There was a sharp metallic click. Strong, jagged teeth dug through skin and crunched against the bones of my right hind leg just below my hock. It happened so quickly that the surprise and shock outweighed the pain. The pain came later—a hot, deep throbbing pain if I remained still. When I moved to try and drag myself free, my whole leg screeched in agony. The gin-trap was securely fastened by a stout chain and iron spike driven into the hard ground. In a frenzy, I attacked it and broke several of my teeth. I tugged and shook it but could not get free. The sky in the East was getting lighter. The bloody hens were poking their ridiculous beaks out of their hut and cackling as though demented. It was barely light and I was still struggling to break the chain or work the spike loose, when I saw, out of the corner of my eye, a large pair of muddy black gumboots and the metallic blue sheen of the barrels of a shot-gun.

The bastard shot me in the stomach so that I'd die slowly. I felt as though fifty red-hot needles were digging into my guts. I tried to vomit. The searing flashes of pain were replaced by cold numbness—then I woke up.

CHAPTER TWENTY-THREE

CLOBBERED BY A COW

MR NORTH'S heifer at Manor Farm was due for her second injection against Wooden Tongue.

I'd rung through to the farm after surgery, to remind them that I was coming and to make sure that the heifer was in, ready for me. There had been no reply.

The farmyard was deserted. I tooted on the horn, changed into my thigh-boots and went in search of Harry. Everything looked clean; there had been a fall of snow during the night which effectively masked the many blemishes.

I found him in the small yard on the other side of the empty bull-pen. He was busy mucking-out one of the calf pens and talking earnestly to himself. Dollops of dung were sailing out through the open door-way. They splattered on to the snow covered yard, staining its virginity.

I coughed loudly; Harry stopped talking and came to the door. He greeted me with a smile, giving me the benefit of his massive, snow-white dentures.

'Have you got her in?' I asked, hopefully.

' 'Course I 'ave,' he answered with pride. 'Come and 'ave a look.'

I followed him past the steaming heaps of calf dung to the feed store, with its dry, mealy floor and neatly stacked rows of food sacks. He fished for his pipe. It was in the pocket of his jacket which he had hung up on the handle of a broom propped against the wall. When he'd got it drawing nicely, and not before, he took it out of his mouth and pointed the stem towards the back of the door.

Printed in three inch high letters in chalk were the words 'Vet coming Toosday 15th'.

'See,' he said. 'I weren't going to forget and mess you about like last time. She's all ready in the box in the other yard.

' 'er's stopped dribbling and I fancy she looks a mite better. But it'll take some time to get something on 'er back. 'E let her go too far.'

'Where is your boss?' I asked. 'I tried to phone up and he wasn't in.'

'Dunno. 'E went orf this morning. 'E ad the trailer 'itched on, so I reckon 'es going to buy some more calves.'

'If you can get me a bucket of water, I'll get the stuff from the car.'

'It'll 'ave to be cold. 'E's too mean to put in a boiler.'

Clutching the injection apparatus, I crossed the yard to the loose-box, slipping and sliding on the hard frozen, vintage cowpats. Harry had her ready tied up to a hay rack. I gave him the 'bulldogs' to clamp into her nose.

I adjusted the length of binder-twine round her neck to bring up the jugular vein. Harry pulled her head round to one side, away from me, so that the skin over the vein was tense. The vein was filling up nicely. I tested it with my finger-tips and jabbed in the needle.

She reacted instantly and violently. Her hind leg, on my side, came up and forward, past the point of her shoulder and cracked down on my thigh. It was only a glancing blow but it knocked me off balance. I collapsed in an ungainly heap in the straw. The effort of her kick threw her off balance too. Having her head pulled round, she swayed over and fell on top of me—all eight hundredweight of her.

A searing pain shot up my left leg. Simultaneously, I felt and heard the hot, tearing crunch as my tibia and fibula broke under the unequal strain. Tears of pain twitched into my eyes and a cold wave of shock, physical and mental, engulfed me so that the pain, though no less intense, became detached. I viewed it momentarily from above and outside myself.

This moment passed, as reality, in the shape of the hot, hairy side of the heifer, pressed my face into the straw which covered the floor of the loose box.

The needle had hit the vein first go. A steady, warm, sticky stream flowed over my ear, round my neck and down inside my shirt.

Harry, with some presence of mind, let go of the 'bulldogs'. The heifer, with her head free, got up with a minimum of struggling, trod on my hand and walked over to the corner of the box. She stood looking down at me with a total lack of interest or concern—I might have been her still-born calf.

Harry was worried. His dentures clacked rapidly.

'You orlright?' he asked.

The searing heat of the pain had subsided to a fierce throbbing which hammered to the accelerated rhythm of my pulse.

We both looked at the leg together. The lower part of it, a few inches above the ankle, was at right angles to the rest. It looked grotesque—like one of those sick party jokes.

'Christ,' said Harry, his mouth dropping open. 'What are we going to do about that?'

'Sit me up first and we'll have a think,' I said, as calmly as I could.

He slid his arms under my armpits and lifted me into a sitting position. The heifer was bleeding steadily from the needle in her jugular vein.

'You better pull that needle out, before she bleeds to death,' I told him. 'Make sure she doesn't kick you,' I added, with a weak smile.

He stood well back from her rested one hand on her shoulder and snatched at the needle. He then opened the loose-box door and drove her out.

'I'll go up to the house and phone for a doctor and an ambulance,' said Harry. 'You hang on here.'

'What do you think I'm going to do? Race you to the house?'

He grinned inanely. 'I'll be back soon.'

Ten minutes later he was back.

'The old bugger's locked up the house. I can't get in to phone. The nearest one's at the Spotted Cow, a mile and a half away.'

'I'm all right here,' I said. 'If you could walk down there, call the ambulance and ride back up in it. Before you go, could you pull me over to the wall. It'll be more comfortable with something to lean against.'

Once more, he took me by the armpits. Stabbing pains shot up my hip and beyond as my angulated ankle caught in the straw. He propped me against the flint wall and lit a cigarette for me. I was sweating so much, I could hardly draw on it.

I was prepared for an hour's wait—I'd worked it out—half an hour's walk in the snow, a phone call, and the time for the ambulance to pick him up and drive on to the farm.

Forty-one minutes later, I heard the sound of an engine coming up the lane.

Harry, beaming, strode into the box.

'Didn't 'ave to wait for the ambulance,' he announced. 'Little Willie was 'aving 'is lunch time pint at the "Cow". 'E brought me back 'ere in his dust-cart an' 'e'll run you into hospital in it now. 'E says 'e'll probably get the sack, but 'e don't give a cuss.'

Standing proudly behind him was Little Willie; his hairy navel peeping coyly over the brass buckle of his belt.

He picked me up like a baby and it hardly hurt at all.

'You better go First Class—in the cab. 'Arry 'ere can ride be'ind.'

Our arrival outside the Casualty Wing of the hospital did not go unnoticed. Willie had fitted an old-fashioned bulb horn to his dust-cart. He used it to good effect.

The Casualty Sister bustled out in response to the vulgar hooting. She looked prim and petulant.

'We don't have collections on Tuesdays,' she announced, firmly.

Little Willie leaned out of his cab.

'This ain't no collection—it's a delivery. The vet just got clobbered by a cow.'

Her face softened a little—though still nonplussed.

'What did you say?' she asked.

Harry jumped out of the jumble of dustbins at the back. He shone his dentures at the Queen Bee and rasped his hand over the stubble on his chin.

'Excuse me Ma'am.' He drew himself up another inch. 'Our veterinary surgeon has just been injured. Can you see 'im. We

185

couldn't get no hambulance, so we brought 'im in this.'

Little Willie had hopped out his side, picked me up and was holding me like an anxious mother.

'Where shall I take 'im?' he asked aggressively.

The Casualty Sister, who, in spite of her job, was human, looked at him, then at my leg. She turned on her heels and said, 'Follow me.'

We followed.

'Put him there,' she ordered pointing to a slab in a room which looked and smelled like a mortuary.

I lay uncomfortably on the hard, cold table. Harry and Little Willie stood to attention by the side of the table, their caps in their hands, as in mourning. The casualty sister shooed them out, but they managed a parting wave to me.

Sister's attention had been focused entirely on my distorted leg. She came up to me, held my hand and looked at my face. It was, no doubt, pale and I was sweating.

She then saw the blood—the heifer's blood—over a pint of it—which had congealed on my ear, all round my neck and soaked into my shirt. She blinked twice and ran across the room. She had her thumb on the panic bell, but kept her eyes on me, as though I was going to run away or just die.

The house surgeon, in his own good time, sauntered in.

'Trouble, Sister?' he enquired loudly.

Sister didn't answer. She just pointed.

I sat up.

'I'm sorry to trouble you but I think I've got a broken leg.'

The Sister was capable, she was used to emergencies. But when I sat up, I think she thought I was suffering from vertical rigor mortis. She even held the house surgeon's hand.

The houseman was different. His pay was so meagre that he was quite divorced from the realities of his work.

'Lie down,' he ordered.

I lay down. The casualty sister relaxed her grip on the house surgeon.

'What seems to be the trouble?' was the next fatuous question.

'I've got a broken leg,' I replied, as levelly as possible.

'Why the blood?' he asked.

'It's not mine,' I said. 'It belongs to some cow.'

He was not amused.

'Take the boots off,' he ordered the casualty sister.

It looked like a very sharp lino knife. It slashed through my almost new and quite expensive thigh boot from top to bottom. My trouser leg was treated similarly. The increased pain induced by this treatment diverted my attention from the loss of my boot and the ruination of my trousers. I then lay untended and apparently ignored, except for a reminder from the Sister that I was not supposed to smoke, to await the pleasure of the house surgeon.

Twenty cold minutes later, he re-appeared and surveyed me with cool, clinical indifference. He then explored the fracture site with his fingers. It was painful and, I felt, unnecessary.

'Take him through to X-ray, and remove that other boot. It's covered in manure.'

One hour and two X-rays later, I was returned to the Casualty Department and anaesthetised, having been asked to name my next of kin.

I woke with a raging thirst and a full length thigh plaster, encasing my left leg. The ward sister asked me how I was and bustled off without waiting for my reply. Tea arrived and, out of desperation, I drank it.

Eileen turned up at the end of the evening visiting hour. She sat on the side of my bed and looked very concerned.

'Are my vast clientele disappointed with my absence from the evening surgery?' I asked her.

'Only one man came in. He wanted some worm tablets for his puppy. I gave them to him and charged him half a crown —was that right?'

'Fine,' I said. 'Nothing else happened?'

'Harry and Little Willie turned up. They got the landlord of the Spotted Cow to drive them up to Manor Farm. Harry collected all your injection stuff and Little Willie drove your car back. They parked it in the yard and took the bus home.'

It felt good to have friends. 'I'll hobble into the pub tomorrow and repay their kindness,' I told her.

187

'The ward sister said you had to stay here for two or three days,' said Eileen.

'The ward sister can go and jump in a bed-pan. I'm leaving here tomorrow morning. I've got work to do.'

It was eight o'clock when I eased myself out of the taxi outside the Spotted Cow. I held on to the door and the driver passed me my crutches. I adjusted them under my armpits, balanced on my good leg and fumbled for the fare.

He drove off, leaving me on the deserted, snow-covered forecourt of the pub. I was fifteen paces or thirty careful hops from the public bar—I was determined to make it. The thick rubber ferrules on the ends of my crutches were not designed for crossing the snow-covered approaches to public houses.

They'd worked fine in the ward—after a few trial runs. The ward sister had chastised me verbally, but with an edge of humour in her voice. I'd kissed her on the cheek and promised to castrate her cat for nothing—and she let me go.

The door marked 'Public Bar' looked a long way away and it was cold outside. Both crutches shot out sideways, leaving me teetering on my one good leg and the old sock which covered the bare toes of my other one. Cold shivers shot up my back as I strove to keep my balance. I felt like a duck on a frozen pond. I hunched myself up, drew in the wayward crutches and started off again.

A loud cheer greeted me as I swung confidently into the warm smoky atmosphere. There were only six in the bar, so I called to the landlord that drinks were on me—they were all drinking beer anyway.

Little Willie and Harry insisted that I join in a game of darts. My crutches were a handicap, but they were also an excuse. These boys were frighteningly accurate with a dart. Normally I would have been ashamed to play with them. As it was, my standard of play was no worse than usual.

Well after legal closing time, they carried me out to the taxi. The taxi driver had been called an hour before. He'd hooted his horn but it seemed a pity to leave him sitting out in the cold, so he was invited in for a quick drink. He helped to carry me out. If I hadn't been on crutches, I think they would still have had to carry me out.

The taxi-driver dropped me outside the surgery.

Nonchalantly, I waved one crutch and fell over. I lay giggling in the snow. There was no pain. He switched off his engine, got out of his cab and tried to lift me up.

A policeman arrived on the scene—they always do. He couldn't have been more helpful. All three of us weaved our way across the broad pavement.

'Have you got your key, Sir?' he asked. With their continued support and encouragement, I found it.

While he was fitting it into the lock, I decided, in all seriousness, to question him.

'What's your name, officer?' I slurred.

'Fletcher—Police Constable Fletcher, Sir.'

'You're not going to charge me, are you?' I whined in a maudlin voice.

'Of course not, Sir'—the accent was firmly on the 'Sir'—'You're merely in need of assistance.'

'Thank you officer. I was afraid that you were going to charge me with being drunk in charge of a pair of crutches.'

Next day I felt dreadful. I could hardly prop myself up at the surgery table. It must have been the after-effects of the anaesthetic.

CHAPTER TWENTY-FOUR

HAPPY CHRISTMAS

THE next four years were the most enjoyable and satisfactory of my life.

There was, first of all, the problem of survival. The prospect of failure, looming ahead like Becher's Brook the first time round, was a challenge. I drove myself harder than I would have driven any employee. The incentive, I thought, was a successful practice with one or more assistants. I was available twenty-four hours a day, seven days a week to each and every one of my clients.

I viewed with envy a neighbouring practice; well-established with a principal and two assistants. They would have nights off duty at regular intervals. The principal could take a long week-end, and leave the work without his practice suffering.

On one occasion when we met, I pointed this out to him. He told me that I should consider myself lucky. He said that he was far happier when he had been working on his own. Now that he had a big practice he had more worry. And even though he had two assistants, he seemed to work harder than he ever had to before. I didn't believe him.

Many times, I was invited out for a day's shooting or a week-end sailing. I had to refuse. My practice was too young to abandon or even to wean temporarily on to an assistant.

Towards the end of the fourth year, the pressure and volume of work had increased so much that I had to consider getting an assistant. There were some days, and nights too, when, being unduly harassed, the standard of my work suffered. It would have been better to have refused work than to accept it and then do it badly.

On Christmas Day work started early. My parents had

come to stay at a hotel in town and I had dinner with them on Christmas Eve, and got back home at midnight. At half past twelve, a few minutes after I'd got into bed, the phone went.

It was one of my good clients. He had two dairies and milked over a hundred cows at each one. One of his heifers, having recently calved, had a prolapsed uterus or, as he put it, pushed out her calf-bed.

It was bitterly cold and raining sleet. He didn't tell me on the phone that she'd calved early, unexpectedly and had not been moved into a loose-box. She was in an open yard, most of which was flooded. She was up to her hocks in freezing, liquid dung. Her uterus, like a bloated red sack, hung down to just about her hocks.

We waded through the manure, got a rope round her neck and coaxed her to the side of the yard where we tied her to the railings.

It looked to be an impossible task to get such a distended mass back inside the heifer. I picked up the adherent after-birth. It needed several buckets of hot water and disinfectant to clean off the mud, bits of straw, etc.

I organised a broad wooden plank and covered it with a clean sheet, supplied reluctantly by the farmer's wife. I then embraced the soggy mass with both arms and eased it up on to the plank. The farmer and his cowman, holding each end of the plank supported its weight. I started to push it back inside her—a formidable task. With every handful I pushed in, she would strain and push most of it back out again. A spinal anaesthetic would have stopped her straining. It would also have stopped her from standing up. As we were all wallowing in over a foot of semi-liquid dung, it would have been impossible if she had lain down in it. It would have been better if we could have driven her out of the yard on to dry ground, but the gateway was flooded to a depth of over two feet.

I worked at it for two hours, with freezing rain stinging my bare arms. I was sweating inside the clammy rubber cover-all, yet my feet were numb with cold. The last bit disappeared inside her. I sorted it out, so that there were no folds or kinks and put a handful of pessaries in to control any infection. We let her go and went back to the farmhouse.

The sweat on my back and chest was now icy cold. I was shivering. Some hot black coffee and a large tot of rum in the warm atmosphere of the kitchen made me feel much better. I didn't want to get up from the table, go out into the cold night and drive home even though it was half past three in the morning. I finally made the effort. I was just going out of the back door when the cowman came in. He looked very glum.

' 'Er's pushed the 'ole bloody lot out again,' he announced.

'And a Very Happy Christmas to you too,' I responded.

The farmer's wife was asleep, so we filched another of her sheets without her consent. I was feeling so depressed after so much wasted effort that I would have bought his bloody heifer and shot her, if I'd had the money.

It was nearly six o'clock when I got back to the surgery. This time I'd stitched her up with a sack needle and strong tape. She was so exhausted that she didn't even flinch and I was so exhausted, I didn't care if she did pee in three separate streams for the next few days.

I didn't bother to undress; I just lay down on the bed.

At half past six the phone rang.

'I'm terribly sorry to worry you so early, but could you come out and see my dog.'

'What's the trouble?' I answered shortly.

'I know it's Christmas Day,' he answered.

'So do I,' I replied.

'Well, Bruce—that's my dog you know—woke me up. He wanted to be let out. Taken short I suppose. So I let him out. He ran across the road just as the milk lorry went by. He seems to be very badly hurt. He's lying on the grass verge and I don't like to move him. Can you come out.'

I went out. At least I didn't have to get dressed first. He *was* badly hurt. He'd obviously got a broken femur—thigh bone—and possibly internal injuries.

He looked at me as only a Labrador can. It was partly reproachful, partly pleading—yet it was neither, because it had a remote yet definite independence that engendered respect. He was a fine character.

I picked him up. It hurt him and he bit me. Strong white teeth clamped on to my wrist. I carried him into the house. His wife, not looking her best in hair curlers and a dull grey nightie, looked at us with distaste. It was obviously her husband's dog.

'Can you do anything for him?' he asked.

'I'll do my best,' I said. 'I'll give him a sedative injection now and take him back to the surgery. If you phone me up at ten, I'll let you know the worst.'

'Would you like a cuppa?' he asked.

'It would be most welcome,' I answered. 'But I'll get my case from the car and give him his injection first.'

'I'm going back to bed. You can make your own tea,' was the sour comment from his spouse. She swept out, metal curlers glinting dangerously in the lamplight.

I put the sedated, soporific dog on the passenger seat and drove back to the surgery, stroking his ear with one hand.

The X-ray showed a clean break across the femur and apparently no other damage. The only way to fix it would be to put a stainless steel pin down the marrow cavity. Quite a major operation.

I put him in one of the large kennels and switched on the heating. I would keep him sedated until the following day. He would then have got over the shock of the accident and there would be less bruising and haemorrhage at the site of the fracture.

I cooked myself some breakfast and was enjoying a cup of coffee and a cigarette when, once again, the phone rang.

It was meant to be a surprise Christmas present for their young daughter. A small black, poodle puppy. It had a broad red ribbon tied in a bow round its neck. It was now no longer a secret. It was lying flat on its side, all four legs paddling furiously in its own pee, its pretty red ribbon damp and bedraggled. Saliva, churned into froth, oozed from its champing and chattering jaws. Hysterical, high pitched yapping completed the sad picture.

The daughter, aged around seven, with her blonde hair tied back with a matching broad red ribbon, stood watching the performance. Her eyes were large, damp and anxious. The hem of her new dress was being twisted into a soggy strand by her hot little hands.

'We left her with the neighbours last night,' explained the mother. 'Daddy crept out this morning to collect her. He was on his way up to Susan's bedroom—he was going to open the door very gently, push the puppy in and shut it again—when it had this fit. It's been going on ever since—it's over an hour now. Do you think she'll be all right?'

It could have been due to teething, worms, tonsilitis, epilepsy, meningitis, encephalitis, lead poisoning, anal glands or even rabies. How the hell was I to know at eighty-thirty on a Christmas morning when I hadn't even been to bed?

To save the daughter and also the parents further mental trauma, I picked up the pathetic, shivering wreck and took it out to my car. It would be much easier to form an opinion as to the cause of its fit in the quiet isolation of my surgery, unencumbered by the distraught humans.

I returned to the house and assured them that I would do everything I could to return their pet in a normal, healthy state.

I took my little black bag and returned to the car. I'd made a mistake—I should have put it on the floor, not on the front passenger seat. It had scrabbled across on to the driving seat and, in veterinary parlance, had defecated liberally, rolled in it and spread it widely.

'Happy Christmas Farrier' I muttered again as I surveyed the sordid shambles, and drove back to the surgery.

The phone rang. 'Happy Chistmas darling.' It was Mother. 'I tried to ring you before, but you didn't answer. I suppose you were fast asleep. That was naughty you know. It may have been somebody with a sick doggie. If you want to succeed, you must give your clients a good service.'

I wished her a 'Happy Christmas'.

'We're having the turkey at lunch time, so be sure to get round here at twelve. We can have a drink before going in to feed.'

'Yes, Mother,' I answered. 'Happy Christmas.'

The puppy's tonsils looked like a couple of red chipolatas. This was encouraging. The fit was almost certainly due to a streptococcal infection. It was curable and there was no reason why it should reoccur. They were nice people and the girl, deprived of her Christmas present, looked so sad. It made me feel much better. If it settled down, I'd take it back that night or Boxing Day at the latest.

The labrador with the broken leg was still heavily sedated. He looked at me with heavy, hooded eyelids. He looked like an incurable alcoholic, but he managed to wag his tail.

I sedated the twitching poodle and filled her full of anti-biotics.

The phone rang. It was a market gardener, a very successful one, who ran a herd of Herefords to augment his supply of farmyard manure. He lived twelve miles away. I'd been lucky with the odd cases he'd called me out to before. He thought I was God's gift to cows and would have no one else.

'Happy Christmas, Denis,' he started.

'The same to you,' I replied. 'Is that all?'

'You must be joking,' he replied. 'Why should I waste good money on a telephone call? It's one of my better heifers. She's been trying to calve for over two hours—nothing's happened and my stockman's worried. So am I. It was A.I.—a nomi-nated bull. Deep-frozen semen—ouch.'

'Has her water-bladder burst?' I asked.

'I don't know. This is Christmas Day—remember—I'm at home. You'd better speak to Bill here.'

I spoke to Bill.

'Happy Christmas Sir. Sorry to worry you today. I'd like you to come out and 'ave a look at 'er. She's been fidgeting about for a couple 'o days now. 'Er water-bags went two 'ours ago. I don't like the look of 'er.'

The roads were icy. As I drove towards the South Downs, the frozen snow on the roads made driving more hazardous.

She was a great big Hereford, waddling around the loose-box on over-grown feet. Relatively speaking, her vulva looked so small, it didn't look as though she could produce a mouse without assistance.

195

Bill produced a bucket of hot water. I took off my jacket and shirt and donned the cold, wet rubber overall.

It was a normal presentation—two bloody great hooves and a wet nose.

I got ropes on to both feet. We pulled and waited and waited and pulled. It was no good being impatient. She was going to calve—with our assistance—but in her own good time.

It was after three o'clock when she gave the final bellow and her first-born was produced. I poked the snot out of its nostrils, rubbed it with a wisp of straw and it started to breathe.

'When you've cleaned up,' said Bill, 'come up home and 'ave a Christmas drink. The missus 'll be 'opping mad. 'Er Christmas dinner all spoilt. It'll make it easier fer me if you come back for a quick one.'

I had two quick ones and then another one. I was invited to partake of dried out, overdone turkey, but it was after four o'clock and my parents were expecting me.

They were asleep in armchairs in the residents' lounge.

'We asked them to keep yours warm for you, but I think it's a bit late now. You'd better have some tea and Christmas cake.'

The tea was like nectar. The Christmas cake was soggy but I ate it, and having promised not to be late for dinner, I went back to the surgery.

The Labrador flipped his tail. The poodle puppy was standing up looking eagerly through the bars of her cage—she looked fine. I didn't feel like taking her home but she was, after all a Christmas present and it was still Christmas.

They were overjoyed. The look in the little girl's eyes was the best Christmas present I could have had. I had to have several drinks before I weaved my way happily back to the hotel.

I was now determined to get an assistant.

CHAPTER TWENTY-FIVE

THE BANK MANAGER

SITTING outside the Bank Manager's office, I felt decidedly apprehensive, rather like a schoolboy waiting to be called into the headmaster's study. I tried to reason with myself—I hadn't committed any crime—he wasn't going to chastise me —all I wanted was some money.

I sat on the edge of the chair, fiddling with the brim of my hat. It was worse than a dentist's waiting room. There were no magazines to thumb through.

The door opened and a worried looking man crept out. He looked at me, averted his eyes and shambled past. I wondered —had he been 'blubbing'—or had he had 'six of the best' or merely a good 'wigging' and a hundred lines. I was beckoned in.

A smile and a box of cigarettes were pushed towards me across the imposing table. I felt less ill-at-ease.

He was prepared, in principle, to allow me a loan. What security could I offer? My good name as a professional man was not good enough. I didn't want to have to fall back on my father but they would accept him as a guarantor, so I had no option. It was made quite clear to me that as everything was fine, they would lend me this financial umbrella but if I struck a bad patch and it started to rain, they would want it back at once.

I was now in a position (or was it a tight corner?) to advertise for an assistant.

I did not word the advertisement in glowing terms. I merely stated 'Assistant wanted, interview expenses paid, salary by arrangement' and my phone number.

I had five replies. It was not an easy task, interviewing prospective assistants. I'd never done it before and I didn't know how to question them or what to look for. I think they were equally uncertain.

The one that made the best impression and appeared the most confident was from the Commonwealth. He was tall, blond and good looking with a pleasant manner. He asked over the phone whether he could bring his wife. I, of course, agreed. She was equally attractive. Both he and his wife had to travel down from Scotland—a long and expensive journey—for which I recompensed them.

I met them at the station. They looked fresh and alert. They told me that they'd taken a sleeper and travelled overnight from Scotland to London. They then caught an early train from Victoria station down to Sussex.

I had three farm visits to do. They came round with me and I was able to show them the surrounding countryside.

I liked his strong accent and his rough and ready manner. He preferred to call a spade a shovel.

He was impressed with the surgery premises and his wife seemed more than satisfied with the accommodation I offered. He approved of the car which I had bought on the 'never-never'.

I then took them on a tour of the town and wined and dined them at an expensive restaurant. We discussed the terms of his employment over lunch.

I had already seen three other prospective assistants and had made arrangements to interview one more, next week.

I decided that this one up to now was the best choice.

I drove them back to the station.

'When can you start?' I asked, as we sat waiting in the station forecourt.

'We're going to Cornwall now, and then to Ireland for a few days, we'll be back the week after next,' he answered. 'I'll think it over and let you know as soon as we get back.'

He let me know, by letter. It was a pleasant letter and he thanked me for the lunch but he didn't think that he would accept the job—it wasn't quite what he was looking for.

I found afterwards that he and his wife had left the country two months later and returned to their native land. They had come over on holiday, to spend three months touring the British Isles and Ireland. What better way than to be shown around and entertained by a succession of veterinary surgeons? I had paid their rail fares from Scotland to Sussex. The next stop had been Cornwall, with the veterinary surgeon there paying their travelling expenses and overnight accommodation. And their next interview was Ireland.

The assistant I chose—or perhaps it was he who chose me—was newly qualified and newly married. A definite asset, from my point of view. He wouldn't be wasting time horsing around with local girls, as I was. And, equally important, when he was on duty, his wife would be available to take phone messages.

He looked older than his years, which was an advantage. Clients, especially farmers, would think that he'd been qualified for some time and that he was experienced. He had a quiet confident manner which again created a good impression.

The Farmers' Ball was one of the best events of the year. It was good for business to meet my clients socially and to be introduced to other farmers. It was also a very enjoyable evening with excellent food. I took the same girl as I had to all the previous dances. She was a radiographer from the local hospital, the one who had X-rayed my broken leg. Each year, I had been lucky and had not been called away to attend any emergency. This year I could relax and really enjoy myself as I had left Peter, my assistant, on duty.

It was the end of February. Freezing hard outside, warm and convivial in the hotel. It was around ten o'clock when we were just about to sit down and feed. The band had, for the moment, stopped playing. Loud and clear through the microphone came the announcement: 'Will Mr Farrier please go to the Reception desk.'

It was Peter, my new assistant. He was ringing up from Pond Farm and he was very apologetic.

'I hate to call you out but I'm stumped. I've been trying to lamb this ewe for nearly two hours. Could you pop over and help?'

I made my excuses to my partner and left her in charge of a gaggle of my farming friends.

'Popping over to Pond Farm' was a twelve mile journey on black, icy roads.

The lambing pen had been constructed out of straw bales along one side of large open stone-walled cattle-yard. A six foot high wall also of straw bales had been built up along the front of them to serve as a wind-break. But there was no wind. It was a still, starlit, icy night.

Peter met me at the yard gate. He looked grey with cold and worn out with his efforts, lying in the straw with a straining ewe for nearly two hours. The ewe looked better than he did. He offered apologies while I was pulling my thigh boots over my evening dress trousers.

'It's like having a dog and barking yourself,' he suggested.

'Not to worry,' I answered, feeling better having made the effort and arrived at the farm. 'It'll be a change from an Old Fashioned Waltz. What's the trouble with her?'

'Both front feet are coming but the head's back and I can't get it round. I'm worn out and the ewe's getting a bit dry.'

'I suppose the bucket of water's cold by now,' I said.

'It was cold when I started. They haven't got any hot water,' he answered. 'And I've run out of disinfectant. Have you got any?'

The wet folds of my rubber cover-all had frozen together. It creaked as I pulled it open. The icy cold struck through my frail white dress shirt. My bottle of disinfectant was useless—it had frozen solid. I couldn't get a drop out and there were no means of thawing it. I smeared my hand and arm liberally with antiseptic cream.

Forming the fingers of my left hand into a tight little cone with my thumb tucked inside it, I slid it up past the lamb's front feet. It was beautifully warm. There wasn't much room, but then there never was inside a ewe. I found the head, hooked one finger into the cleft between its lower jaw bones and pulled it straight. I kept my finger in its mouth to guide it, pulled on both front feet with my other hand and out popped a lamb. It was pretty weak but it was still alive. It had taken me less than five minutes.

Peter was astounded and embarrassed.

'I've been messing about for nearly two hours and you come along and do it in five minutes.' There was admiration yet an undertone of resentment in his voice. 'I feel such a fool calling you away from the dance for such a trivial thing.'

'It wasn't a trivial thing,' I reassured him. 'I've been lambing ewes for years—even before I went to College. I used to help the shepherd on my uncle's farm. You'll get the hang of it in time.'

He accepted my explanation and looked happier.

The dance had not collapsed because of my absence. In fact they all looked slightly merrier than when I left them. They'd saved me some food but it was cold. I returned to the bar and made a brave effort to catch them up.

Next morning, I left Peter to cope with the surgery, while I did the outside calls. As I was feeling a little fragile, I felt that the fresh air would do me some good.

My first call was to castrate a six-week old litter of piglets. A nice simple job requiring no great mental effort.

The piglets had not been weaned and were still running with the sow, who was a bad tempered old cuss. It would have saved a lot of time and effort if the farmer had enticed her away from them at feeding time and kept the piglets shut in ready for me. Using large sheets of plywood, we ushered the frisky little piglets into their wooden house, and shut them in, leaving mum outside. The boundary of the run was a single strand of electrified wire.

The sow had, once or twice, made contact with the wire. She was now extremely wary of it. Even though we switched off the current and opened up one section of the wire, she was frightened of crossing the line. With some coaxing and a little bullying, we eventually got her out. We then joined up the wire and switched on the current again to keep her out.

The farmer eased open the door of the pig-house and crawled in, while I held the door shut. After a lot of squealing and thumping, he passed me a piglet by its hind leg. It was a gilt so I let it go. It scampered under the wire to join its mother. He picked out all the gilts first, so that the sow would have something to occupy her mind and would be less likely to try and attack us when the squealing really started. When we had finished castrating the boar pigs, we had another struggle to get the sow back into the run. A few handfuls of pig-nuts helped, but she was still a little chary.

We had re-connected the wire and switched on the current, when a man, well dressed in a tweed suit with a boxer dog at his heels, strolled over to join us.

'I heard the squealing, so I thought I'd come and see what was happening,' he announced.

'This is the wife's brother,' said the farmer by way of an introduction. 'He's come down from London for a few days, to teach us how to farm. You're a bit late Harry. We've just finished. We could have done with your help earlier.' He then winked at me. 'While you're here though, you can make yourself useful. Just pull that bit of wire tight, will you?'

Harry ostentatiously re-adjusted his pipe in his mouth, bent down and grasped the wire. As the voltage shot through him, he jerked backwards and dropped his pipe. He retrieved it from the slushy mud and stood shaking the pins and needles out of his arm. His brother-in-law was vastly amused, but Harry was not. He stuck his pipe back in his mouth, took it out again, spat, wiped the rest of the pig-manure off the stem and stalked off.

His dog, sensing his master's discomfiture, stalked aggressively up to one of the small posts supporting the electrified wire and lifted his leg in derision. As the stream of pee hit the wire going over the insulator, the current shot back up it. The effect was electric. His other hind leg, with a convulsive kick, left the ground. He did an acrobatic front-paw stand, toppled over sideways and went yelping down the field after his disgruntled master.

'What did you do that for?' I asked the farmer, with some sympathy for Harry and his dog.

'He's a prick,' was the short answer. 'How much do I owe you?'

Another of my calls was to a local riding stable. It had a sleazy atmosphere. Sloppy, teenaged girls hung around the place. I reckoned that they didn't only use the hay for feeding the horses. They had a pony with acute laminitis or fever of the feet. This condition normally occurred in over-weight ponies on a lush spring pasture. It was not to be expected in half starved nags in the middle of winter.

It was led out of its stall, hobbling painfully, its hind-legs tucked well underneath it, to ease the weight off its front feet. Both fore hooves were hot to the touch and the merest touch with a hammer caused it to rear up in pain.

I questioned them as to its feeding and was told a pack of lies. I found out later that they were fed on straw, a little hay and the odd handful of rolled oats. This pony had broken into the feed store and eaten half a bag of high-protein nuts, reserved for their one and only show-jumper.

After weeks of treatment and skilful attention by the 'Shooey', who made and fitted surgical shoes, we got him going sound—even at the trot—though he went a bit 'pottery' in front. The soles of both front feet had dropped and I warned the owner that, although he could be used for work, he could never be sold with a certificate of soundness.

CHAPTER TWENTY-SIX

A CAESAR

THE pressure of work was increasing every week. I had planned to take a holiday but it was impossible for me to leave Peter on his own, even though he was competent. I looked back with nostalgia to the days when I had first started and life had been leisurely—conveniently forgetting the worry and the gnawing uncertainty as to whether I was going to succeed. I had succeeded—I thought. Anyway, I was busy—frantically busy. And I had an assistant—something I had often dreamed of in the earlier, uncertain years.

I could forgo my holiday, even though I'd only had an odd week-end off during the last five years. Peter was entitled to three weeks' annual holiday. It was written into his agreement, as was the condition that he would not start up in opposition to me within a five mile radius for five years after leaving my employment. What was not written in was that, if he was due for an evening off duty and I was very busy, he would help me—but he always did.

I had to get a locum to help me out over his holiday time. It was easier than choosing an assistant. Only one answered my advertisement. I had to pay him nearly double Peter's salary and Peter was still getting his salary while on holiday. I also had to hire a car for him as Peter wanted his to enjoy his well-earned time off.

We managed. Even though he was older than me, which put me at a slight disadvantage. He made a few mistakes, but so did I.

I persuaded the locum, with suitable reimbursement, to stay over an extra day. I was going to have a long week-end in Paris. He'd be on his own the whole of Saturday and Sunday. Peter would join him for the usually hectic Monday and I would return to the fold, ready for work on the Tuesday morning.

Friday night, with a slightly apprehensive sigh of relief, I drove up to London Airport—a free man, for seventy-two hours.

At nine-fifteen on Tuesday morning the phone rang. It was Lady Flowater.

'I bought a new pony for my daughter last Saturday. We had the blacksmith along yesterday to check its shoes. He tells me it's a cripple. It's got dropped soles and it'll never be sound.'

I was feeling fine after my long week-end. I assumed a smug voice. 'That was a little careless of you. Wouldn't it have been wise to have had it examined for soundness before you bought it?'

'I did,' she answered abruptly. 'Your locum examined it on Saturday morning. I have his signed certificate here. May I read it out to you?' A deep, heavy feeling settled in my stomach.

'This is to certify,' she continued, 'that I have today examined the above described pony. It is sound in wind and limb.' There was a pause. 'What do you think I should do?' she asked innocently.

'How much did you pay for it?' I asked, knowing I was caught.

'Seventy pounds,' she answered, in a flat, uncompromising tone.

'I'll come up at lunch time and see you,' I replied, as graciously as possible under the circumstances.

'I shall expect you,' she answered, and rang off.

I went to the bank and increased my overdraft by seventy one pound notes—I felt they looked more impressive than fourteen fivers.

I phoned up the 'wide-boy' at the riding stables. He was not available. He'd done a moonlight flit that weekend.

I handed over the money to her Ladyship, mounted the pony and rode off. It was much to small for me and I felt slightly ridiculous.

I rode over to the yard of my old acquaintance—the horse dealer from the market. I tied the pony to the ramshackle gate and picked my way, once more, but on a different errand, through the tangled wire to his line of stables.

Once he'd seen the pony trotted up, there was no question of bargaining. He had me by the short hairs. I hadn't a leg to stand on and the pony only had two good ones. He was not exactly generous but he gave me three fivers, which was better than nothing. I knew its slaughter value would be over twenty pounds.

The pressure of work continued to increase. I could still cope with it, though I tended to get short-tempered at times. It was not fair on Peter however and he seemed to be getting restless and dissatisfied.

The following Sunday, he was off duty. It was ten o'clock in the evening, when Alan Reid rang up from Meadow Farm. He'd been sitting watching one of his Guernsey heifers trying to calve since lunch time. As she was a heifer he didn't expect her to be too quick about it. But I wished he'd called me before.

I'd been thinking hopefully that I would have a quiet night and was toying with the idea of going to bed early. I drove out to the farm and examined her. I then drove back to the surgery and started preparing the instruments for a caesarian. I rang through to Peter's house—there was no reply. I'd done caesarians on my own before, but it was hard work and one's efficiency was reduced and therefore the risk to the cow increased.

While I was waiting for the instruments to finish their boiling session, a car pulled into the yard. I feared that it was another case. A car door slammed and I waited. Peter poked his head round the door.

'Busy?' he asked. 'I'm T.B. testing early tomorrow, so I thought I'd collect all my stuff tonight. What have you got on?'

'A caesar. You couldn't have come at a better time. I tried to ring you ten minutes ago and there was no reply.'

Peter's face fell.

'We've been out to dinner. I dropped Peggy at home, and

told her I'd only be a few minutes collecting my stuff. I'll have to ring her and tell her what's happened. She won't be very pleased.'

'Thanks,' I answered. 'I hate doing this to you but it's a hell of a job single handed, as you know. I'll whip off now and start to clip and shave her. You can follow with the instruments when they're ready. I've already given her a shot of tranquilliser.'

'Why has she got to have a caesar?' he asked.

'Because there's a dirty great lump of bone sticking up from her pubic symphysis. Although her ligaments have slackened off, she hasn't opened up at all. She'd have a job producing a rabbit, let alone a calf. She must have split her pelvis at some time.'

'What did the silly bugger want to stock her for. He must have known she'd have trouble calving,' said Peter, in a disgruntled voice.

'I don't suppose he knew. They don't use Artificial Insemination, they've got a bloody great Guernsey bull and he's too heavy for the young heifers. When she was served, she probably went down under his weight, straddled her legs and split her pubic symphysis. The farmer probably wasn't watching and if he was, he wouldn't have appreciated her problem. She'd walk as though she'd wet her knickers for a few weeks and he'd think she'd just strained herself. When it healed, it left this large bony callus sticking up and the whole pelvis is rigid.'

'What are they going to do with her afterwards? There won't be any point in breeding her again—the same thing will happen.'

'If they don't stock her again, she'll probably milk on for a couple of years. When she's dry, they can fatten her up a bit and sell her for meat. She's got nothing on her at the moment. If they send her for slaughter now, they won't get much for her and they'll lose the calf. If she milks really well as a heifer it might pay them to stock her again and have another caesar.'

'If they do stock her again,' said Peter, with feeling, 'let me know when she's due and I'll take a long weekend off duty.'

By the time Peter arrived at the farm with the instruments, I had finished clipping the hair off a wide area of her flank and was busy shaving a patch of skin, twelve inches wide by two-foot-six long, with a safety razor which kept getting clogged up with hair.

The heifer was lying comfortably on a bed of clean straw. A metal framed inspection light had been rigged up and was suspended from a beam in the loose-box roof, so that it hung over and illuminated the operation site.

Peter stood watching me for a few minutes. 'Are you going to give her a general or do it under local anaesthetic?'

'We'll use local; paravertebral nerve block. You can start on that now if you like, while I finish the shaving.'

He clipped and cleaned off five areas of skin, just lateral to the heifer's backbone. Using a three and a half inch long needle, he injected local anaesthetic into each site, deep enough to block off the sensory nerves before they entered the vertebral column and joined up with the spinal cord.

Alan Reid had been watching the proceedings from the doorway, with a look of concern on his usually jovial face.

'Why are you injecting her there?' he asked.

'To anaesthetise the whole area of her flank where we're going to operate,' Peter answered.

'Aren't you going to chloroform her then?'

'No. Chloroform's too dangerous. If we wanted to give her a general anaesthetic, we'd use chloral and give it into her jugular vein. There's less risk with local, both for the heifer and the calf.'

'What's to stop her getting up and walking away, halfway through the operation?'

'She's had a fair dose of tranquilliser so she probably won't feel like standing up. We've done one or two standing up, but it's much more trouble for us. A calf can weigh over a hundred pounds and it has to be lifted up and out of the incision. Much easier when the cow's lying down on her side.

'This is a nice quiet heifer. She won't feel any pain and I think you'll find that she'll behave herself. If she was wild, we'd give her a spinal anaesthetic as well. That would paralyse her hind legs so she'd have to lie still.'

I finished the shaving and cleaned and disinfected the skin. Peter had laid out the steriliser and the rest of the equipment on straw bales nearby.

Before giving the operation site its final application of antiseptic, I prodded the area with a needle to test the efficiency of the anaesthetic. There was no response from the heifer, so all was well.

We put on our operating gowns and spent five minutes scrubbing our hands and arms with disinfectant soap.

The operating cloth was a single linen bed-sheet with a rectangular hole cut in the middle. This was draped over the heifer's flank so that the hole coincided with the shaved area.

With a new blade fitted on the scalpel, I made a sweeping incision, eighteen inches long, through the thick skin which twitched and gaped open. A few small arteries squirted blood and were clamped off.

Alan, who had been watching closely, took a few paces backwards and continued to watch from the doorway, while I opened the abdomen by cutting through the muscle layers and peritoneum.

Laying aside the scalpel, I inserted my hand and arm, and felt around in the warm darkness. I could feel the calf and traced my hand round the curved and distended uterine wall until I found one of its hocks. I held on to it and with my other hand, grasped the foot of the same hind leg. With considerable effort, I lifted it up and out through the incision.

I held it while Peter packed large gauze swabs between the edges of the incision and part of the uterus which contained the calf's hind leg. He then cut through the uterine wall. Fluid gushed out and was absorbed by the swabs. He grasped the exposed leg and pulled it out. It gave a vigorous kick and he nearly lost his grip on it. He found the other leg and by holding on to both gently eased the calf up and out of the incision while I held on to the cut edges of the uterus.

Being a Guernsey calf, it only weighed around sixty pounds, but it was dead weight and awkward to handle. He dragged it across to Alan. It was a heifer calf, which would please him, and it was blinking its eyes and snuffling. It had a good chance of surviving. We got him to give it a brisk rub-down with straw.

I continued to support the uterus while Peter removed the cleansing. It separated without much difficulty. Had it been too firmly adherent, we would have left it inside and removed it a couple of days later through the normal channels.

The uterine incision was sutured with catgut. The peritoneum and muscle layers were similarly closed. The skin was sutured with strong braided nylon.

From the first incision to the final stitch, it had taken us two hours; most of it occupied by closing the various layers in the long incision.

The heifer was still lightly sedated and was chewing absent-mindedly at some hay, being quite unconcerned with our activities at her other end. The calf was lying down but had lifted its head and was looking around in wide eyed curiosity. We picked it up and laid it in front of its mother. She stopped chewing and looked at it with suspicion. She then gave it a tentative sniff, lowered her head and bunted it out of the way. She resumed her chewing and from time to time eyed her calf with distrust.

'After the handling it's had, it smells too much of us and not enough of her,' we explained to Alan. 'It's bound to be a bit strange for her. Especially as it's her first calf. She may be willing to accept it if we camouflage our smell. If she doesn't you'll have to stay with her for a while to see she doesn't injure it.'

I picked up the afterbirth which was lying in a soggy heap in the straw, rubbed it over the calf's head and body and draped a bit of it over its chest. We then pulled the calf back under its mother's nose, stood back and watched. She gave it a suspicious, sideways look again, paused and sniffed at it. She sniffed again, then started to lick it.

'We're away,' said Peter. 'She'll take to it now all right.'

CHAPTER TWENTY-SEVEN

THE IMMACULATE BITCH

I'D charged Alan twenty pounds for the caesarian on his heifer. Peanuts for the amount of work involved, but if I'd quoted him a higher price, it would have been uneconomical for him to accept and he would have had her slaughtered. From the time I had first gone out to try and calve his heifer, driven back to the surgery, selected and sterilised the instruments, completed the operation—with Peter's skilled assistance—and finally returned to the surgery, well over four hours had elapsed.

Peter's evening off duty had been rudely interrupted and his wife further antagonised against the stress and uncertainty of country practice.

I gave Peter a five pound note as compensation for his disturbed evening and in appreciation of his willing and necessary help. My expenses for the whole operation were twelve pounds. The income tax on my eight pound profit was three pounds six shillings. So it worked out that I'd spent over four hours on a Sunday night, exercising my professional skill for a net loss of six shillings.

The next day, I offered Peter a partnership. He refused—for the same reason that I had turned down Bill and Mike's offer. I was too young. He didn't want to be a junior partner for the rest of his days. He'd stay with me for a while but when he did leave, he wouldn't go into country practice. He'd either put up his plate in a big town and confine himself to small-animal practice—far less dangerous and far more lucrative—or join the Ministry of Agriculture staff. With them, he'd get a five day week, three or four weeks' holiday a year, extra days off at Christmas and Easter and a pension at the end. In small-animal practice, he wouldn't be spending his

211

time wading through snow, ice and other things in the middle of the night with little or no financial advantage to himself.

He could do a caesarian on a bitch in under an hour, in the warmth and comfort of a surgery, and if it was a valuable pedigree bitch, get twenty-five guineas for his efforts—most of it net profit.

He was getting a lot of experience with me and the work was often interesting, so he didn't mind carrying on for a year or two, knowing it wasn't for ever.

His wife wasn't happy. She didn't see much of him and when she did, he was tired, dirty and often smelling of ripe and ancient cleansing. She wanted him to get a nine-to-five job with every weekend off.

Although the work increased, the overheads also increased. I was now working at full capacity and making far less profit than I did when I was on my own. The only consolation was having every other Sunday off, if Peter wasn't too busy.

Being in demand, an established and appreciated member of the community, I felt I had to expand and progress.

Once more, I waited, hat in hand, outside the Bank Manager's office, to plead financial support for a second assistant.

I'd paid for the second car—now I needed a third. I was still in my tiny flat over the surgery. Peter and his wife had far superior accommodation, on which I'd paid off little more than half the mortgage. I now had to tie another mill-stone round my neck. Equally good or better accommodation had to be provided for the next assistant—they were harder to get now.

Reluctantly, God, in the shape and sombre suit of the Bank Manager, granted my requests.

I had two replies to my advertisement; one of them was from a woman veterinary surgeon. If I had not been in country practice, I would certainly have chosen her, not for her looks but for her ability and dedication. But my farming clients would not have accepted her. They were mainly old-fashioned and conservative. They didn't think it right for a mere slip of a girl to go round castrating bulls. Looking on the practical side, there would be times when she would not have had the physical strength to manipulate a difficult calving case. She might

212

find herself trying to control a ten hundredweight, awkward steer, when the farm labour available was inadequate or bloody useless. There were times when brute strength was indispensable. I had to choose the man. His starting price was higher than Peter's present salary even though he was less experienced.

Though there was too much work for two of us, there was not enough to keep three fully employed. I was doing less and less veterinary work, which I liked, and more and more office work, which I hated. The turnover did increase but the profit margin dropped even further.

The interest on my massive loan from the bank had to be met. Rates paid, by me, on three separate properties. Car insurance and tax on three cars to be found, plus allowance made for their depreciation, which was considerable when they were being driven over rough farm tracks, by assistants who were always in a hurry. Every quarter, I had to cough up the mortgage repayments—after tax. Then there were the insurance stamps, higher drug bills and breakages.

The holiday problem was solved. Two of us could run the practice for a few weeks. I took three weeks off. The first holiday I'd had for seven years. I couldn't really afford it, but I put off paying one of the larger drug bills.

Peter, in the nicest possible way, gave me three months' notice. His wife had finally persuaded him. If I hadn't got a replacement for him at the end of three months, he said that he'd stay on until I was fixed up. I offered him a further rise, which I could ill afford, but he was not to be tempted.

Another advertisement, more interviews and salary fixing. The most difficult thing with a new assistant was getting him accepted by the farmers. By the time they were accepted and knew their way around the countryside, they wanted to leave. A few clients were very awkward and refused to accept an assistant—it had to be me. So, with two new assistants, I had to work far harder than either of them. I didn't even have time to worry about my overdraft.

The Bank Manager took care of that.

Once more I sat outside his office. This time it was different—he had asked me to come and see him. I knew why.

'Good morning, Mr Farrier. Do sit down.' This time he didn't offer me a cigarette. 'There don't appear to be enough funds in your current account to meet the interest payments this month. And the quarterly repayment on the mortgage also falls due this month. What are we going to do?'

I was a country vet, not a business man. I didn't know what the hell we were going to do.

'I don't know,' was my lame reply, as I closely examined the patterns in the wood grain of his polished desk.

'WE can't go on like this you know.'

'I could get rid of one assistant,' I suggested. 'I could then sell his car and flat. Would that help?' I asked.

It was a retrograde step which I resented, but I appeared to have no option.

'That would seem to be the best thing to do,' he replied. 'Think it over and come back to me next week. I am responsible to my directors, you know,' he added kindly.

I thought it over during several sleepless nights. I thought back to my conversation with my neighbour, who had since died. I remembered him telling me that he was happier when he was on his own, without the worry of assistants, and that I should consider myself lucky. I hadn't believed him then. Now I wished that he was still alive so that I could tell him how right he had been.

I thought back to the days when I had time to spend evenings in the public bar of the Spotted Cow, with 'Harry the teeth' and Little Willie. My dart throwing had improved considerably, though I never reached their standard or became eligible for the pub team. It was many months since I'd had the time to look in even for a quick one and I missed the relaxed and easy going atmosphere of the public bar.

I decided that I would not sack one assistant. I would sell up—lock, stock and barrel.

I thought about joining the Ministry of Agriculture but I didn't think I could face a nine-to-five administrative job even with the prospects of a pension.

I decided to go back to square one. I'd put up my plate

somewhere else, start again on my own and stay that way.

I knew I'd be happier and less harassed, both socially and financially, working on my own. The next time I would not worry if I had several quiet days. I would appreciate them to the full. The next time, I would try and restrict the growth of the practice by charging higher fees and refusing to work for awkward clients and bad payers. The next time, I would call the tune. If, in spite of my efforts, it still continued to grow, then I'd sell out again.

Having made up my mind to stop being an inefficient business manager and to start, once again, being a country vet, made me feel a lot happier.

I felt quite nostalgic about my last appearance in the surgery. The sell-out had been a financial success. I could now face my bank manager without cringing. The challenge of starting again, a little richer and wiser was a good thing. One client remained in the waiting room. I called her in.

She looked like a wire-haired terrier gone wrong. Mainly white with black and tan patches. A hairy little bitch, with kind eyes. The owner was less sympathetic. I had verbally chastised her about two years earlier for allowing her bitch's dew-claw to grow round into its pad. It must have been very painful and she spent most of her time licking it. She had been left with this painful condition for over two weeks. I resented this neglect and had told her so in straight Anglo-Saxon terminology.

I don't know why she came back to me—but she did. Her small son, aged around eight, came with her. She lifted her bitch on to the surgery table and said she was constipated.

'For how long?' I asked, remembering the last episode.

'Only this afternoon. She started straining at lunch time and can't seem to pass anything.'

I stroked her head and let her lick my ear to give her confidence.

'Is she off her food and has she vomited?' I asked.

'No. She seems quite normal otherwise.'

Her small son decided to join in the conversation.

'Mummy. Why don't you like Mr Farrier?'

215

A swift frown. 'Shush Darling, we're busy.'

'But Mummy,' he insisted. 'You *said* you didn't like him.'

'How old is she?' I asked.

'Seventeen,' she answered, with a brittle tone.

'That's not a bad score. And she was all right until lunch-time?'

'She seemed to be fine. I didn't notice anything wrong.'

I felt her tummy. She had some enlargement of the mammary glands and I could squeeze out some milk. She also had a clear, watery vaginal discharge. I thought I could feel a puppy's head. With the stethoscope, I could hear the rhythmical ticking of a foetal heart.

'She's pregnant,' I announced. 'She's trying to produce a puppy and I think it's stuck. That's why she's straining. It's not constipation.'

'Absolutely ridiculous,' she exploded. 'She's seventeen years old. She can't be pregnant. We tried to breed from her when she was two years old—that's fifteen years ago. She wouldn't have anything to do with the dog. She wouldn't let him near her. After that we didn't bother. Every time she's been in season we've let her run around and nothing happened. She can't be pregnant.'

'Then she must have changed her mind,' I answered. 'Some girls do.'

'I don't believe you.'

'Then I suggest you take your immaculate bitch elsewhere. It's up to you. She will have to have a caesarian if she's to survive. If you leave her, she'll die. It's your bitch and it's up to you.' I lifted her off the table and placed her gently on the floor. I would have liked to tell Eileen to call in the next client, but there wasn't one—this was the last.

'What shall I do then?' she asked.

I gave her a stony stare and remained silent.

'What shall I do then?' she repeated.

'Madam. You can do just what you like. I am a veterinary surgeon. You have come to me for advice. I have given you that advice. You don't have to heed it. That will be ten shillings please.' I closed my case up.

216

'Do you think she'll survive an operation?'—the tone was now softer.

'She's an old bitch,' I answered, looking her straight in the eyes. 'There's bound to be a risk. If you now want me to try I'll do my best.'

'How much will it cost?' she asked.

I thought of a number and doubled it. She didn't complain.

It was a bitch pup and it was alive which pleased me greatly.

She was a different woman after she'd seen the result of the operation: one live and squeaking bitch pup.

For fifteen years she had been disappointed by her bitch's inability or unwillingness to breed. Now she was like a proud grandmother. Not only did she pay her bill, she actually thanked me.

'What about the stitches?' she asked.

'You will have to bring her back here in ten days time to have them removed.'

I didn't tell her that I wouldn't be there.

CHAPTER TWENTY-EIGHT

A PLACE IN THE SUN

I WANTED a place in the sun. Too often I had been called out of a warm bed on wintry nights to face frozen roads and snow-drifts to work in the numbing cold of an ill-lit barn.

I looked south towards the Mediterranean. It was surrounded by people who varied in their approach to animals from callous indifference to active cruelty. None of them was a good prospect for a veterinary surgeon wishing to earn a living, apart from a sprinkling of ardent pet-loving expatriate British.

Almost in the centre of this limpid sea are the Maltese Islands; Malta and her small sisters Gozo and Comino. They are inhabited by people more ethnically variegated than the British—Phoenician, Arab, Turk, Berber, Sicilian, Greek, Spanish and Italian who have, to quote Ernle Bradford, 'cross-fertilised this area during the last 2,000 years'.

Few of these races in the pure state have much concern for household pets and their welfare, yet these jumbled genes have produced a tightly-knit group of people—hardly a nation, more like a club—quixotic and over-proud yet more sentimentally involved with their animals than the most rabid, vociferous British so-called animal lover.

As with the British, some of them throw out their unwanted puppies and kittens. Yet there is no more cruelty to animals in Malta than there is in Britain and considerably less cruelty to children. Children can roam the streets without fear of molestation. They will be guarded and cherished even by strangers. There is no need for an organisation like the NSPCC. In most cases animal suffering is caused by thoughtlessness and acts of omission. Rarely is it intentional.

Dog-fighting, though illegal, is a popular pastime in Malta

—possibly copied from the British, who for generations bred dogs specifically for this purpose.

The contestants are massive-muscled animals weighing between eighty and one hundred pounds with their ear-flaps cropped right off to prevent them being torn in battle—it also gives them a sinister expression. They are tough professional bruisers showing in their conformation the influence of bull-mastiff, boxer and doberman. Their jaws can crush the thigh-bone of a sheep in one short savage crunch.

I am frequently called in to tend to the losers. Their necks, forearms and cheeks are covered in bites—tiny little pin-prick wounds, most of which do not penetrate through the skin. Two dogs fighting in the street will inflict the most appalling injuries on each other. These professionals are far more careful and considerate towards each other. The noise and action are spectacular and, as in all-in wrestling, they give good value for money.

Though the human inhabitants of Malta are of very mixed blood, there are two types in the indigenous canine population which have remained pure and bred true for hundreds and even thousands of years.

The Kelp tal Fenek—literally 'the dog of the rabbit' has changed little from its image of Anubis which decorated the tombs of the Pharaohs, three to four thousand years ago. They still pose like Anubis with their fore-legs extended and their large bat-like ears pricked attentively. In other countries they have been mutated into greyhounds, whippets and salukis but in Malta after several thousand years they remain true. In England they are known as Pharaoh hounds.

Oddly enough a few wild rabbits still survive in these rocky islands through the parching heat of summer. Small peasant farmers go out at night with a pair of these dogs and a torch, coursing rabbits. It has little in common with the Waterloo Cup. It is more like a crazy old-fashioned steeplechase. Savage, rock-strewn gullies dotted with stunted fig and carob trees, prickly-pear cacti with needle-sharp spines and liberally sprinkled with rusted tins, broken bottles and war-time barbed-wire. It makes a constant source of income for a veterinary surgeon prepared to do needlework.

As with the greyhound and especially the whippet, they have no protective coat, their skins are soft and thin and they tear like tissue-paper. Involved in the chase, they run as fast as greyhounds and, in their enthusiasm, have little concern for their personal safety. Large triangular torn flaps of skin hang on them like macabre Christmas decorations.

At any time between ten and midnight, the phone or the doorbell will ring. A man brings in his bleeding dog. He also brings his family and several friends for good measure. It is not only idle curiosity—they love that dog and are fearful for its future. Their faces are set in mourning, which implies little confidence in the veterinary surgeon of their choice.

The owner is loath to watch his own dog being anaesthetised and sutured so he delegates one of his friends to stay and witness the assumed execution. It is not only that they think that the dog might die under my hamfisted surgery. They are suspicious that it might live and that I will sneak it out through the back door, tell them it had died and then sell it to someone else.

Having been stitched up, it now looks more like a dog and less like a rag-bag. The owner is summoned in by his friend. He is no doubt happy to see his dog alive and looking present-able but he is careful to show no pleasure. The small peasant farmer has little enjoyment in his hard life and I think he has forgotten how to smile. If he remembered and felt inclined to show gratitude, he would control it severely as it might adversely affect his position in the bargaining that was to come.

In England, a professional man states his fee and expects to receive it without demur. If he charges too much, his client might grumble to himself and seek other advice in the future. Seldom does he haggle and attempt to bargain over the price as he might in a street-market.

My client is dressed in his normal working clothes—thus he starts with a considerable advantage. His trousers are frayed and torn—even the patches have patches. Broad, flat, horny feet are set obstinately on the floor with black cracked toenails looking like small dirty shovels. Shoe leather wears out, his thickened soles repair themselves and he can stride over flint-sharp rocks without pause.

As with the shoes, it appears that he cannot even afford to buy a razor blade. How can I possibly charge this poor old man anything? He watches me to see whether I have penetrated his disguise. His eyes have a deep-set cunning inherited perhaps from his astute Phoenician ancestors and which enabled his fore-fathers to survive hundreds of years of Arab domination. How can I compete against this accumulated duplicity? I have turned out at night, performed a reasonably skilled professional operation on his dog, including the anaesthetic and antibiotic injections. I think it is worth four pounds and like a fool I say so. He is rendered speechless. For a moment it looks as though he is going to faint. He wipes the gnarled back of his hand across his furrowed brow. He is obviously overwhelmed by the monstrous demand I have made on him. He looks to his family and friends for moral support. They have been well rehearsed in their supporting role and look suitably aghast. Tentatively he moves forward his pawn: He 'didn't think it was going to cost more than a pound'. I exaggerate the cost of the anaesthetic and drugs used. He counters this adroitly: 'He only paid three pounds for the dog'. I fumble the next move by referring to the professional skill involved. It cuts no ice. Check-mate—virtually fools-mate. 'If I'd told him it was going to cost so much, he'd have shot the dog and not brought it to me.' I accept two pounds. Reluctantly and with a martyred expression he pushes his hand into his trouser pocket. The wad of notes, mostly fivers, is so thick it brings out the patched lining of his pockets. I have to give him three pounds change.

The Maltese terrier, in spite of its name, has to take second place to the Tal Fenek. Its history goes back for some 2,000 years when it was mentioned by Aristotle more than 300 years before the Christian era and by Strabo (63 B.C.—A.D. 21). An ancient name for Malta was Melita. There was another island in the Adriatic called Melita and Canis Melitaeus may well have its origins there. It has altered little since described by Aristotle. Its small size and long, fine silky coat made it a favourite pet of the ladies of Imperial Rome. Though still a lap-dog in Independent Malta, it has an alert manner and a pleasant character. In spite of its diminutive size it seldom has trouble whelping unlike the Maltese type chihuahua which is a recent import to the island. These chihuahuas with their distorted domed heads and small pelvic bones are a constant source of trouble at parturition and frequently call for a caesarian. A tiny monument to man's stupidity and greed—the smaller the dog the higher the price.

There is a fourth dog indigenous to Malta. A most likeable character that looks like a cross between a beagle and a pointer, yet breeds true. It is called the Kelp tal Kacca—the dog of the hunter.

On first arriving in Malta, one is struck by the almost complete absence of bird-song. The still, calm early-morning hours are uneasily silent. Anything and everything that flies gets shot and even a sitting bird is not safe from these trigger-happy so-called sportsmen. Those that avoid the guns are often trapped in nets, having been lured towards them by one of their fellows caged as a decoy.

The efforts of responsible Maltese citizens to curb this senseless slaughter have, to date, not been attended by any great success. More enlightened countries kill off their birds with pesticides and industrial pollution. Yet here, in spite of their old-fashioned methods of shooting and trapping, they have been remarkably successful in eliminating practically all bird life. This success is not necessarily due to accurate shooting but more, one feels, to the intensity of the gun-fire. The island of Malta covers an area of 95 square miles. There are 10,000 licensed guns. So that every square mile can offer a concentration of over 100 guns.

In April, thousands of birds, mainly quail, migrate from North Africa to Europe. During this month, from the first light of dawn and continuing for several hours, one is under the impression that there are far more than 100 guns per square mile, all being handled with zest if not with skill. Occasionally, yet all too infrequently, they shoot themselves. This does not appear to diminish their ardour. To walk in the country in April and September is extremely hazardous. Anything that moves is shot at. The noise is terrifying. Spent shot and shot not fully spent rain down on house and garden, windows and nerves are shattered.

In Cairo everybody was a bird-lover and amateur ornithologist. They photographed them, wrote letters to the papers and urged the government and the RSPCA to take all possible steps to protect them. And at week-ends, the complete British male population of Cairo would sally forth with 300 cartridges apiece to the marshes lying to the north and south-west and happily exterminate every bird they could see.

In Malta, nothing is spared. Sparrows and skylarks, warblers and wagtails are literally blown to pieces by these enthusiastic sportsmen. Tired out after their long migratory flight they see Malta as a refuge and resting place—and they don't stand a chance. The survivors are caught on their return journey in September as they migrate south for the winter. The advent of the automatic shotgun more than compensates the inaccuracy of the marksmen.

Exhibited, unfortunately with pride, in private collections are the shot and stuffed specimens of birds who have foolishly visited these islands. The variety is intriguing: pelicans, osprey, flamingoes, cranes. A golden eagle and a wren. A kite, a buzzard and a golden oriole. Many diving birds, herons, ducks and a cuckoo. It is a sad and sorry sight.

My Maltese gardener is a good gardener. He is a quiet, solid, reliable countryman. He tends and prunes the vines, orange and lemon trees and they fruit well. He makes asparagus grow as if it was a weed. He is fond of animals and especially so of his own Tal Kacca. He keeps canaries and is distraught if one dies, though his grief may be tinged with a little Arabic fatalism—it is the will of Allah. He is not wealthy yet he owns a very expensive five shot automatic twelve bore and spends a lot of money on cartridges. When he is carrying that gun he is metamorphosed into one of the 10,000 licensed bird slaughterers.

He once caught a parakeet. Somebody's pet, a cagebird which had escaped. It had not had an easy life playing truant and its bright green and red plumage was dull and bedraggled. He nursed it until it had recovered its brilliant hue and sheen. He then let it go and as it flew away he shot it. He showed it to me with pride; stuffed and mounted with his many other specimens in a glass cabinet.

It is nearly midnight. The outside air temperature is 78°F. The water in the swimming-pool is 85°F. I am floating on my back, looked down on by the large bright stars in a blue-black sky. My horizon is limited by the ten foot high dry-stone walls of the garden erected many years ago to protect the orange trees from the salt-laden winds. Strands of bougainvillea and heavily laden vines blot out some of the stars. An anonymous cat goes straight up the side of the wall with an easy liquid movement and picks its way sedately along the top.

The Maltese cat—not a recognised breed but a distinctive type, is, I think, unique. They have enormous bat-like ears and attractive pointed faces. They come in all colours—black, white, tabby, ginger and tortoise-shell. They are sleek yet athletic and rangy and they talk Siamese. When they walk and they do so disdainfully, it appears as though they were walking downhill as their hindlegs are considerably longer than the front. A useful asset in a country criss-crossed with high walls. One assumes that those with normal hindlegs faced with a ten foot high wall and pursued by dogs failed to survive.

'Ponce'—one of ours—a young undoctored male Maltese, flows down from another wall, picks his way aristocratically across the 'boule' pitch and looks down on me (floating in the warm water) as though I was mad. With studied nonchalance he flicks his tail and stalks off towards the patio to join 'Pimp' his dad—another Maltese though darker and more heavily jowled.

If he thinks I'm mad, who cares?—I'm happy.